D0998695

THE KING PENGUIN BOOKS

61

AN ATLAS OF TUDOR ENGLAND AND WALES

AN ATLAS OF TUDOR ENGLAND AND WALES

FORTY PLATES FROM
JOHN SPEED'S POCKET ATLAS
OF 1627
INTRODUCED AND
DESCRIBED
BY
E. G. R. TAYLOR

PENGUIN BOOKS
LONDON

THE KING PENGUIN BOOKS

Editor: N. B. L. Pevsner
Technical Editor: R. B. Fishenden

Published by Penguin Books Ltd,
Harmondsworth, Middlesex, England,
Penguin Books Inc, 3300 Clipper Mill Road,
Baltimore, Md, U.S.A., and
Penguin Books Pty Ltd, 200 Normanby Road,
Melbourne, Australia

This volume first published 1951
Reprinted 1953
Made in Great Britain

Text printed by R. & R. Clark Ltd, Edinburgh
Plates made and printed by
John Swain & Son Ltd, Barnet

AN ATLAS OF TUDOR ENGLAND AND WALES

A FAITHFUL MAP and description of his Kingdom is something not unworthy the contemplation of a Monarch. Charlemagne himself counted three great maps engraved upon silver among his treasures. So said John Leland, Library Keeper and Antiquary to Henry VIII, when relating to his royal master how in the last six years he had collected material out of which to write fifty or sixty books descriptive of the Realm. 'Now if it shaul be the pleasure of Almighty God (he wrote) that I may live to performe these Thinges, that be already begune and in a great Forwardnes, I truste that this your Reaulme shaul so welle be knowen, ons payntid with his natives Coloures, that the Renoune thereof shaul gyve place to the Glory of no other Region.' A young scholar from Cambridge, Leland entered the King's service in 1533, and five or six years later was commanded to ride on horseback through the length and breadth of the Kingdom, in order to recover or record what was possible of the books and manuscripts which had been scattered, stolen, lost or destroyed during the recent dissolution of the great monasteries: 'a strange and miserable havock' as a later book-lover said. And to this enquiry Leland added not only a search into the genealogies of the nobility and gentry among whom he found entertainment, but a minute examination of the countryside, as he moved from town to town, from castle to manor-house, even on one occasion from manor-house to 'vile cottage' – but this was in Wales.

But Leland's county topographies were never written, nor his maps drawn, for he shortly after became mentally deranged and after some years' illness died in 1552. His friend Reyner Wolfe, the

Royal Printer, was in possession of much of his material, but he too died before he could print it. Various copies of Leland's notes and sketch-maps subsequently passed from hand to hand, to be plundered by this writer and that, and becoming more and more illegible and tattered, until finally what remained was rescued and printed in the days of Queen Anne. Before Wolfe's death, however (in 1571), the times had become more propitious for English map production. New cartographical techniques that had been perfected in Germany and the Netherlands were brought into England, and young men of mathematical bent found employment as land surveyors, drawing large-scale estate plans which henceforth accompanied terriers or adorned the chambers of the landed gentry. It was one of these 'land-meaters', Christopher Saxton of Dunningley, Yorkshire, who was commissioned to carry out a measured survey not simply of a manor but of all the counties of England and Wales. Here would be maps fit for a Queen, and Elizabeth graciously approved the project, granting Saxton the Royal Warrant to travel through the realm, ascending church towers, hills and other vantage points, locating boundary marks, and so on. Even more important, the scheme had the patronage of Thomas Seckford of Woodbridge, Suffolk, who had opened his purse to the young surveyor. Hence this project did not founder on the rock of finance as did so many succeeding ones.

As map-engraving was so young an art in England most of Saxton's county maps had to be entrusted to Dutch engravers. Business relations between London and Amsterdam were then very close, and the latter city was developing a notable cartographical school. Meanwhile, with Saxton's help, and that of material (including Leland's) left behind by Reyner Wolfe, William Harrison, although he himself had never been more than forty miles from home, wrote a *Description of England* prefaced to Holinshed's *Chronicles,* published by John Wolfe in 1577. Nine years later (1586) William Camden produced his famous work *Britannia* which, so his enemies declared, was merely an unacknowledged borrowing from Leland, a charge not completely unfounded. Towards the close of the century two fresh schemes for county topographies were put forward. That of John Norden, like Saxton an estate surveyor, naturally placed the emphasis on new maps, to be accompanied by descriptive text. It started well, but only a few counties were completed, the expense being beyond the author's resources. The second scheme, that of John Speed, by profession a tailor, by inclination an antiquary, had eventually a better fortune, for Speed was satisfied to adapt existing maps to his purpose, and so save the expense of new surveys. At first, however, he met with disappointment. The patronage of Fulke Greville enabled him to present his plan, together with some maps, to the Queen, but the date was 1598. Elizabeth was old and unhappy, and gave him no encouragement.

Just at this time, perhaps by no mere coincidence, one of the Amsterdam school of engravers, Pieter van den Keere, then aged about 28, produced a set of miniature English County Maps based on those of Saxton together with some small maps of Scotland and Ireland of similar type. A year or so earlier he had engraved a number of plates for the first world pocket atlas, the *Caerte Thresoor,* published by B. Langenes, to which his sister's husband, the famous cartographer Jodocus Hondius, had also contributed. His wife's brother, Petrus Bertius, was also interested in publishing a pocket atlas, for there was a rising demand for cheap miniature editions of costly folios. Hondius was engraving the large maps for the folio edition of Speed's *Theatre of the Empire of Great Britain,* which finally appeared in 1611, but whatever may have been first intended, his brother-in-law's small maps were not used for a 'contracted' edition until 1627. Meanwhile, however, another member of the Amsterdam family circle published a pocket edition of Camden's *Britannia* (which had quickly gained a European reputation) and this was illustrated by Pieter's maps of 1599. Some alterations in the plates made for the 1627 issue, which is the one used in this book, hardly altered the content of the maps. Latin titles were merely changed to English ones, and some counties which had been grouped together were redrawn separately. In all essentials, therefore, we have a set of Elizabethan county maps. The frequent mis-spelling of names is a blemish, but one only to be expected from foreign workers. Necessary omissions from Saxton's originals were made on the principle that the space should be neatly filled. Hence tiny villages and inconsiderable 'gentlemen's seats' may be found marked in sparsely peopled country while elsewhere quite considerable towns are left out. Hills or mountains may disappear altogether, or a single conventional symbol do duty for a range. So, too, a single tree must pass muster for a forest, while there was no room for the innumerable 'pretty brockets', the tumbling tributary streams and rills which Leland lovingly described.

In seeking to conjure up the beauty of the Tudor landscape from a few names and symbols upon a map, we must constrain our eyes to the Tudor viewpoint. All but a negligible minority of Englishmen were then country-bred, and discovered loveliness only where they could discern fruitfulness. They perceived no romantic beauty in wildness and solitude; to be barren was a disfigurement, so that they could describe the Lake District as 'cumbered with mountains' and 'pestered with copped hills'. William Harrison even railed at the splendid close-fenced deer-parks with their fine oak timber, their herds of fallow and red deer among the bracken, seeing them as land filched from the plough, for by his day hunting had become a mere sport instead of a necessary means of furnishing the table. The ideal of landscape beauty was that of the cultivator who rejoices to see the valley standing thick with corn, the grass knee-high in the meadows. Such scenes of plenty were to be found at their best in places like the Vale of Holmsdale, the Vale of White Horse, the Vale of Belvoir, the Golden Valley of Herefordshire: these the Elizabethans praised, for they offered satisfaction for every human need. On the upper slopes and hill-tops the woodland and waste provided mast for the swine, summer grazing for the flocks, timber for firing; spread apron-like over the lower slopes and valley floor, the great open fields of arable land provided each man with his strips; alongside the river the carefully ordered water-meadows furnished precious hay, which carried the breeding stock through the winter. A line of clear springs breaking out from the hillsides fixed the sites of the villages, while at some river crossing, a bridge or ford, stood the market town.

Not every landscape, of course, could conform to this ideal pattern – topography forbade it. Furthermore, when Leland rode through England the manorial system was already breaking up, and the self-sufficient parish, if indeed it ever existed, was vanishing before a greater variety of agricultural enterprise adapted to new social and economic needs. All too many districts, as he describes them, were already scant of wood, ancient forests were sorely decayed, and the poor had to burn turf, furze or ling, or even cow-dung for fuel. This was especially so where soils were poor or where charcoal-burners and iron-smelters were at work; there were many blow-furnaces in the Weald, Staffordshire, Warwickshire, and Gloucestershire. Mining and metal-working were on the increase, the new ocean trade meant more shipbuilding, while the expanding population (approaching four millions), and the growth of towns, increased the need for firing and for timber for housing. Fortunately coal had already come into use for the forge and the bake-house; in London (to the disgust of the housewife) even for the domestic fire; but coal could be brought only where there was water-carriage. Moreover, it could not be used for smelting. Round the salt-wiches of Worcestershire and Cheshire, too, coppice wood had been cleared for miles to heat the great evaporating pans.

But if woods decayed, hedgerows with all their charm were extending. Even in the Shires and the Home Counties, where once the open-field system had been universal, enclosures were being made. Some were the work of prudent landlords who found it more profitable to rear sheep than to grow corn, others were made by men who believed in improvement, for experts deplored strip cultivation: 'The countrie enclosed I praise, The tother delighteth not me'. New holdings, too, were being steadily carved from wood and waste (often to provide for the squire's poor relations), and these were hedged in to keep out wandering deer and grazing stock, while in the West country, beyond Dorset and towards the Severn, the fields had always been enclosed, as also in much of Kent and Suffolk and in northern England. Cider apples were planted in the hedgerows of Herefordshire, and in the deep and narrow lanes of Devonshire, bordered by hedge-upon-wall, a rider might stretch out a hand without dismounting to gather wild strawberries as sweet as the famed fruit in the gardens of Somersetshire.

Variety was to be found also in the field crops, since differing climate and soil forbade uniformity: in Lancashire and the Pennines, for example, the peasants ate oaten-cakes instead of the standard wheaten or rye bread. In Leicestershire beans were grown on such a scale that the strong sweet smell from the fields destroyed the scent of hounds, and the Leicestershire yeoman, because of his supposed diet, was twitted with the rude name of 'bean-belly'. Kent already had its cherry orchards, the trees set out in orderly rows, Essex its pretty saffron fields, Pontefract its liquorice (for Pontefract cakes), Worcestershire its perry pears growing by the wayside: nearly every county had its speciality. Industrial crops, flax, hemp, rape and cole-seed, were grown only in small quantities, and with natural reluctance by peasants who knew they must starve if there was insufficient corn. Productivity, and hence general prosperity, fell off towards the north-west and the west; a majority of the four million inhabitants of Tudor England lived on the English Plain. It was a common saying that if an ox could choose his home it would be towards the north, if a sheep, towards the south, while a man would prefer the middle parts – the Shires and Home Counties. Some of the richest cattle pastures were to be found in Staffordshire and South Lancashire, while the chalk uplands of Dorset, Wiltshire and Hampshire echoed to the bleating of sheep. Northampton folk claimed that theirs was the ideal county, 'an apple without a core or rind to be pared away', while others found a very paradise in Middlesex.

The pleasant noises that were as much part of the Tudor land-scape as sights and scents have almost vanished within living memory: the slow creak of waggon-wheels, the clatter of the water-mill, the grind and rattle of the sails of the high-perched windmills, the soft rush of pigeons' wings as the flock wheeled above the manorial dove-cot, the cackle of geese on a thousand commons, the faint elfin call of hunting horns, accompanying the baying of hounds of every degree; and the varying cries, proper to each breed, by which dogs were urged to the chase.

We are linked especially closely with Leland's *Laborious Search for England's Antiquities,* made four centuries ago, by the great landscape change which we are now witnessing. For he saw the first coming, as we now see the passing, of the great country mansions, set in lovely and elaborately designed gardens, parks and pleasaunces. Some of these sprang from the very fabric of the splendid monasteries and abbeys which had been suppressed only a few years earlier, so that he conversed with abbots, priors and monks lodging in the neighbourhood of their lost homes. Those buildings that were attractive and conveniently situated were purchased from the King by the new rich and the newly ennobled of the day to be transformed into manor-houses, while those which lay remotely or attracted no buyer were stripped of their valuable lead roofs and dressed stones so that they fell almost immediately into ruin. Down in the West country, where wool merchants and cloth-makers were acquiring great fortunes, some abbey buildings and friaries were even bought for warehouses and workshops. William Stumpe, the Malmesbury clothier, the wealthiest man in North Wiltshire, took the lead in purchasing the Abbey for a parish church, but put his looms into a side-chapel and into the monastic offices.

But the fate of still older buildings engaged the royal antiquary's attention even more closely than that of the monastic houses. What had become of the famous Barons' castles of feudal England? Save on the Scottish Border and along the Channel these had long outlived their function. Some, Leland noted, had been completely modernized and transformed into comfortable dwellings. Others were represented only by three or four 'mean farmers' houses' adapted from the decayed courtyards and out-buildings. Others, again, had fallen to even lower uses. Where only the thick walls survived, cattle were folded in the castle garth. Even this was not the end. In many cases all that remained was a heap of masonry overgrown with bushes which had collapsed into the dungeons below, and now afforded holts and earths for badgers and foxes. Where such visible evidence was lacking, Leland still made shift, from slight inequalities and discolorations of the ground, to trace the site of some vanished stronghold. But often he was completely baffled. Diligent enquiry of aged men brought no information. A great castle had vanished from sight and memory, save for the words on some faded parchment.

Not every great house which in the 1540's beautified the Tudor scene was either a transformed monastery or a modernized mediaeval castle. There were plenty of plain, solid, old-fashioned manor-houses which had merely been added to or altered to suit the new demand for more comfortable living – here a brick chimney to replace the old 'lantern' in the great hall, there a new gallery or a 'lightsome chamber' – perhaps even a little book-lined study. And many new mansions were being built, especially in metropolitan England, in styles no longer cramped by the necessity for defence, or by the scarcity of such materials as window glass. Yet the architect still thought in terms of towers and turrets, of inner and outer courts and stately gate-houses. These could now be more gracefully built, but they were still the hallmarks of a nobleman's dwelling.

The countryside, however, had no monopoly of new and attractive building. Besides the rich clothiers in the west, there were wealthy maltsters, ale-brewers and meal-men in the Home Counties, prosperous butchers and graziers, merchants and shippers, physicians and lawyers, who could afford to build themselves handsome houses, with ample gardens behind them, along the high streets and cross-streets of the county or market town. Such men, too, when they grew old, bestowed secular benefactions where their fathers had endowed chapels and chantries. Covered pillared markets, such as the lovely ones still to be seen in Wiltshire and the Cotswolds, free grammar schools, almshouses, and above all stone bridges, were their gifts to their native towns, as Leland repeatedly noticed. As business men, obliged to travel, they saw the advantage of replacing a dangerous ford or slow, cumbersome ferry by a bridge, even if it were only wide enough for a pack-horse, and many towns owed their prosperity to such a bridge.

A man on horseback moved more easily about Tudor England than is sometimes supposed, for it was heavy waggon and coach traffic (which had hardly begun) that cut up the roads. Paved causeys were laid where the highway crossed a belt of clay, and were raised on arches across riverside meadows liable to flood. But they were not designed for wheeled traffic. Heavy or bulky goods, such as timber, stone, coal, grain, malt, hay and straw, reached the larger towns by water – indeed, a town that lacked water-carriage could scarcely become important. Harrison declares that there were a couple of thousand wherries and small boats for passengers on the Thames, besides huge tide-boats, tilt-boats and barges for goods traffic. These were matched, though in less proportion, on the Severn, Trent, Yorkshire Ouse, and a score of lesser rivers, so that wharf-men and boatmen were an important section of the population. And the rivers were loved, too, both for their pastoral beauty and for their fruitfulness – their harvest of fish.

THE ENGLISH COUNTIES

For convenience of reference these are
alphabetically arranged

In fine, the ENGLISH KINGDOM (PLATE I), said an Elizabethan, 'is the masterpiece of Nature, performed when she was in her gayest humour; which she placed as a little world by itself, by the side of the greater, for the diversion of mankind; the most accurate model, by which to beautify the other parts of the Universe'.

PLATE 2: BEDFORDSHIRE

'In Bedfordshire is naught to lack' ran the old saying. For although the soils in the south were somewhat lean by comparison with those of the fruitful Ouse and Ivil Valleys, they produced a barley which was plump, white and strong, so that the Luton and Dunstable maltsters drove a rich trade at the London market. The myriad larks that sang on Dunstable Downs and by Whipsnade also found their way, as a potted delicacy, into London larders. 'As plain as Dunstable road' had become a proverb, for the town stood on Watling Street, the most frequented highway in England.

PLATE 3: BERKSHIRE

'Barkshire fill-the-wain' its natives called the county, for although the sandy east part was 'downright barren', the western vales teemed with wheat and barley. From Windsor Great Forest and the Great Frith, near Maidenhead, oak and other timber was shipped down the Thames to London. Between Winterbourne and Newbury stood Donnington Castle, the birthplace of Chaucer, a building 'small, but very neat, seated on the brow of a woody hill, having a fine prospect, and windows on all sides, very lightsome'.

PLATE 4: BUCKINGHAMSHIRE

Hill and vale in Buckinghamshire are matched to perfection, and the county had 'naught to lack'. The Chilterns have altered little – chalky hills covered with woods and groves of beeches – but when Camden looked down from their summits upon the wide and clear prospect of the Vale of Aylesbury he saw a landscape without hedgerows 'almost all unenclosed and marvellously fruitful, its sheep the finest and biggest in all England'. Two generations earlier

Leland had noticed the old house at Chenies being 'translatid' into the newer fashion of brick and timber by the Lord Russell.

PLATE 5: CAMBRIDGESHIRE

'The soile doth differ both in ayre and commoditie: the Fenny is surcharged with waters: the South is Champion and yeildeth Corn in abundance, with Meadowing-Pastures on both sides of the River Cam̃, upon whose east banke the Muses have built their most sacred seat.' The Fens, although aguish, abounded in pike, eel and duck, the water-fowl so cheap, said an ancient writer, that five men could be satisfied for one halfpenny. Of all this wild plenteousness the Drainage was to make an end.

PLATE 6: CHESHIRE

'Better wed over the mixen than over the moor' their fathers told the Cheshire maidens. For in this pastoral county a great dung-hill indicated a man's wealth, a moorish soil spelt poverty. 'The Champion grounds [wrote John Speed] make glad the hearts of their tillers; the Meadows imbrodered with sweet-smelling flowers, and the Pasture makes the kine's udders to strout [that is to say, "bulge"] to the paile, from whom and wherein the best Cheese in all Europe is made.' The brine-springs of the Weaver Valley helped the making of Cheshire cheese; Nantwich and Northwich, where the salt was extracted, were handsome, prosperous towns albeit dirty because of their trade.

PLATE 7: CORNWALL

Atlantic gales, sweeping over Cornwall, cleansed the air 'as with Bellows', and the vigorous Cornishman was famed for his valour as a wrestler. So much so that 'to give a Cornish hug' meant to bring a man to a fall. And according to the poet

> 'Twere needless to recount the wondrous store,
> Vast wealth and fair provision for the poor.
> In fish and tin they know no rival more.

Here was occupation for the landless cottager, in many counties a burden. The fish were pilchards which under the name of *fumados* 'fed the Don of Spain', since they lacked a local market. The tin went abroad or to the London pewterers, after being carried to Liskeard, Truro, Lostwithiel or Helston for weighing and stamping; for an impost of 40s. on every thousand pounds weight was levied on behalf of the Dukes of Cornwall.

PLATE 8: CUMBERLAND

The Derwent, famous for salmon fishing, drains Lake Derwent-water. 'Upon the side of this lake, in a fruitful field, incompassed with wet, dewy mountains and protected from the north winds by Skiddaw, lies Keswick, a place long since noted for mines.' Queen Elizabeth brought Germans into the Lake District to open new copper mines. Near Workington, Camden tells us 'the ancient, knightly family of the Curwens possessed a stately castle-like seat, and from that family (excuse the vanity) I myself am descended on the Mother's side'. There were many such castle-like seats in Cumberland where the squire sheltered his tenants and their possessions from Border raids. Carlisle itself was seated between Eden, Petterel and Caude Rivers, 'and beside these natural fences, it is fortified by a strong stone wall, a castle and a citadel'. From Carlisle there ran a still older defence work, the Picts' Wall, marked on the map by Waleton and Wallton, and so to Wallsend.

PLATE 9: DERBYSHIRE

Two Derbyshires were divided by Derwent, one low and fruitful, having many noblemen's houses and parks; the other, the Peak District, 'all rocky, rough and mountainous; consequently barren, yet rich in lead, iron and coal'. In Dovedale, Camden found nothing to admire, he only saw 'a few country villages', while in the Upper Derwent there was nothing besides Chatsworth, 'a large, elegant and admirable structure'. His taste is echoed in the verse he quotes:

> Nine things that please us at the Peak we see;
> A cave, a den, and hole the Wonders be;
> Lead, sheep and pasture are the useful three;
> Chatsworth, the Castle, and the Bath delight;
> Much more you'll find, but nothing worth your sight.

The 'Bath' was at Buxton where Lord Burghley went for his gout. Here the Earl of Shrewsbury, owner of Chatsworth, had erected lodgings for gentlefolk, with promenades and amusements for those taking the cure, besides a physician in attendance.

PLATE 10: DEVONSHIRE

Tradition has it that Brute, legendary founder of the British nation, made his first landing in Devonshire, at Totnes on the Dart. And from this point the ancient Fosseway was said to start and run to Caithness. It passed through Exeter, which Leland described as a city still strongly walled, with many watch-towers. These walls were a mile and a half in compass, but there were already suburbs shooting out along the main roads, especially towards London; for ribbon-development is nothing new. The river Exe rises in Exmoor, in Tudor eyes 'a filthy, barren ground near Severn Sea', though a rearing-place for young stock. But Devon was traditionally 'mighty and strong', a home for heroes. Leland stood upon Plymouth Hoe, 'a right goodly Walke without the Towne', and marked the great roadstead, the chain and citadel defending the Haven.

PLATE 11: DORSETSHIRE

This favoured shire boasted that it had need of no other. It could feed itself upon its own wheat, fish, flesh and fowl: clothe itself with its own wool and broadcloth: house itself sumptuously with its own Portland Stone, Purbeck Marble and timber. Even foreign luxuries were provided, for the secluded Isle of Purbeck was a favourite landing-place for pirates, where not only the Dorset gentry but the Keeper of Corfe Castle himself used to bargain and buy. It is true that the best hempen rope in all England was manufactured at Bridport near by, but English pirates did not hang – they lived to become national heroes.

PLATE 12: CO. DURHAM

In the Pennines which fringe West Durham, the Tudor traveller found the fields naked, the woods few, the hills bald. He turned with relief to the plains where he could enjoy a landscape 'enamelled with meadows, pastures and cornfields, thickset with towns and abounding with coal'. Moreover, coal was very cheap because, wherever water-carriage was wanting, it could find no market more than six or seven miles from the pit. The stout little donkeys and pack-horses could carry only a couple of small bags, and the cost of transport quickly became prohibitive. The glory of County Durham, then as now, was Durham City, although its spires have vanished. 'The town stands high, and so is very strong; it lies in a kind of oval form, enclosed by the river on all sides except the north, and fortified with walls. In the south part, almost where the river winds itself back again, stands the cathedral church, which with its spires and tower steeple makes a noble shew.'

PLATE 13: ESSEX

Essex, said an old rhyme, was 'full of good housewives', perhaps because it was full of good things – fat Waynflete oysters, shrimps and cockles from the Thames, ewes'-milk cheese from Canvey Island, fish and fowl from the creeks, venison from Waltham Forest. Prosperous clothiers, many of them refugees, lived in and about Colchester; the Thames-side villages were favourite homes for mariners; while courtiers, lawyers, writers and others who had business in London occupied the manor-houses. From the tiny village of Billericay four persons were to sail in Stuart days in the *Mayflower*.

PLATE 14: GLOUCESTERSHIRE

Gloucestershire lies about the lower Severn, which enters it at Tewkesbury, noted for smart-biting mustard, and winds through rich meadows to Gloucester, 'beautified with many fair churches, and handsome, well-built houses'. 'Gloucester, shoe and nail' was its traditional description, for smiths and naylors, as well as clothiers, were among its prosperous citizens. Below Gloucester the Severn meets the incoming tide, and is swept back twice daily, 'raging and foaming like the sea'. Overlooking the wide vale, the steep front of the Cotswolds rises seven or eight hundred feet in height. Summer comes late and hence the saying, 'Long in coming as Cotswold barley', although when it did come it was as excellent as the fine-woolled sheep. On the far side of Severn the Royal Forest of Dean also stood high above the plain. It still supplied the naval shipyards, in spite of the blow-furnaces on its margin, 'the only bane of oak, elm and beech'.

PLATE 15: HAMPSHIRE

Henry VIII secured the passages of Solent and Spithead by a line of strongholds such as Calshot and Hurst Castles. Hampshire still remembered Norman William with reproach, who

> Towns, fields and Churches took from God and man,
> A spacious Forest made in Beaulieu plain,

for the New Forest was no beauty spot to land-hungry peasants, although it nourished a notable breed of pigs. But the Isle of Wight, warm and sunny, a protective bastion against storm and invasion, had corn and to spare to send inland, and to victual outgoing ships. Fine fleeces, too, inferior in softness only to those of Lemster, came from the Island, not to speak of 'store of conies, hares, partridges and pheasants'. Winchester is the glory of Hampshire, where the bones of King Alfred were laid. But Camden, by profession a schoolmaster, had an eye for the 'neat College which William of

Wykeham built for a public school, and which sends out a great number of learned men into Church and State'.

PLATE 16: HEREFORDSHIRE

Where the waters of Teme, Lug and Wye come tumbling out of Wales, to creep over the Hereford Plain, they open gateways which the Lords Marchers stopped with great castles, Brampton Bryan, Wigmore, Clifford, and many more. There were castles, too, in towns in the heart of the county, such as Hereford and Lemster. All these were in decay in Tudor days when half Wales could claim kinship with the royal house. Centuries earlier the Romans had chosen much the same sites to hem in the Silures. At Kentchester close to Hereford the country folk picked up their coins which they termed 'dwarf money', and could point out among the tumbled stones the Chair of the 'King of the Fairies'.

The pastoral landscape of Herefordshire was seen perhaps at its best in the Golden Valley of the Dore where so recently had stood a great abbey. 'The hills that incompass it on both sides [says Camden] are cloathed with woods; under the woods lie cornfields on each hand, and under those fields lovely and fruitful meadows. In the middle, between them, glides a clear and crystal river.'

PLATE 17: HERTFORDSHIRE

Described as 'destitute of nothing that ministereth profit or pleasure for life' and convenient as it was for London, Hertfordshire abounded in noblemen's seats, such as Hatfield, Ashridge, Gorhambury, vanished Theobalds. The last was new built by 'that Nestor of Britain, the right honourable Baron Burghley, Lord Treasurer of England; a place than which [says Camden] nothing can be more elegant: and as to the gardens, walks, and wildernesses, nothing more pleasant'.

When we remember that on all those occasions when we drink tea, coffee or cocoa every Tudor man, woman and child drank beer, the importance of barley is easy to understand, especially round swollen London. Royston on the northern border of Hertfordshire was a typical market, lying on the highway to Ware, the shipping point on the Lea. Camden thus describes the bustle in the thronged streets and inns at Royston on market day: 'It is almost incredible [he says] what a multitude of corn-merchants, malsters and the like dealers in grain weekly resort to this market, and what vast numbers of horses, laden with corn, on those days fill all the roads about it'.

PLATE 18: HUNTINGDONSHIRE

Like neighbouring Cambridgeshire this county had two natural divisions, Upland and Fenland, the latter unequalled for its fat pastures used for summering horses and cattle. The Upland, as we read in Camden, 'is mighty pleasant, by reason of its swelling hills and shady groves. The river Ouse washes its south parts and decks it with flowers', while the entire scene 'as if contrived on purpose by some painter, perfectly charms the eye'. Deep in the Fens, on a tongue of firm ground near Botsey, the rich and famous Ramsey Abbey used to stand, which once sheltered the children of King Canute. It was he who built the causey to Peterborough across the spongy ground. The air of the Fens was damp and aguish, but this was forgotten by monk and peasant alike in the thought of the illimitable abundance of fish and fowl provided without any man's labour on Ramsey and Whittlesey Meres.

PLATE 19: KENT

Every returning traveller knew Dover Castle high on the Kentish cliffs, and the road over Barham Down to Canterbury. Thence he would ride through the narrow street of Sittingbourne, cross the Medway under the walls of Rochester Castle, and strike the Thames at Gravesend. Here, if he was wealthy, he would leave the jolting horse-litter or waggon for the comfort of his private barge, and be rowed past Greenwich Palace where Queen Elizabeth was born, past the storehouses and victualling yards of Deptford, past seafaring

Rotherhithe to London Bridge. The river Medway, after 'passing with a violent course under Rochester Bridge', opened out to carry serenely on its bosom the Royal Navy, 'the best appointed fleet that ever the sun saw', victorious over the Armada. Near its source stood Penshurst, the seat of the Sidneys, home of Sir Philip, 'the great glory of that Family'.

PLATE 20: LANCASHIRE

In Tudor days the London food-market already interested farmers in the remotest parts of the Kingdom. Droves of the huge-horned oxen from the ever-green pastures of Lancashire travelled south to the butchers. But the Lancashire gentry for the most part stayed at home, living still in their 'good old self-contented plainness and simplicity', untouched by that 'luxury, usury, debauchery and cheating which [so Camden said] had brought so many of the old nobility of Southern England to ruin and decay'.

Manchester, with satellite Salford, already dominated Lancashire, surpassing all the other towns for 'building, populousness, manufacture, market place and church'. Liverpool was as yet only just becoming known as a shipping port. Wigan seems strangely described as 'neat and plentiful', but its bright burning cannel coal was already giving light as well as heat in dark cottages. In the north beyond Preston vast moors and mosses 'sore destitute of wood' left the peasantry in great straits for fuel, and the herds of goats among the rocks spoke also of poverty and deprivation.

PLATE 21: LEICESTERSHIRE

'Leicestershire full of beans' – the old saw goes back at least to the fourteenth century; so this was a pleasant-smelling county. On the hither side of the Soar, stretching away to the lovely Vale and Castle of Belvoir, the landscape was open, hedgeless, with but scanty timber, its sweet, nutritious pastures famous for long-woolled sheep and fine beasts. Beyond the Soar, past Leicester City, lay the great Leicester and Charnwood Forests, besides numerous finely wooded parks – Groby, Beaumanor and the Great Park of Cold Overton where the Lord of the Manor (greatly to his profit) was selling pit-coals to his neighbours four hundred years ago. Exactly on the western boundary the Fosseway crosses Watling Street, the spot marked with a High Cross and so named, although when under Queen Elizabeth Protestant feeling ran high a mere post was substituted. Not half a dozen miles away in one direction stands Lutterworth, where John Wyclif was parson, and at the same distance in the other the bloody field of Bosworth where King Richard was slain.

PLATE 22: LINCOLNSHIRE

English Holland was a part of the Fenland which before the seventeenth-century drainage was 'so terribly assaulted on one side with the ocean and on the other with the mighty flood of water from the upper country, that all the winter they watch it, and can hardly defend themselves with banks against those dangerous enemies'. In spite of all vigilance disastrous floods did occur, and one such calamity was fresh in memory when Camden wrote. The silt land near the coast had long ago been reclaimed, but the peat-land behind it was still a vast swamp across which the Fenmen strode on stilts, or pushed through the reeds in little boats called skerries to milk their cows or visit the duck decoys which they termed their cornfields. Even in the upland parts of Lincolnshire the number of wildfowl was amazing, 'and these not the known ones, teal, quails, woodcocks, pheasants, partridges etc., but such as no other language has names for, and are so delicate and agreeable, that the nicest palates and richest purses greatly covet them, viz: puits, godwits, knots, and dotterels so called for their doltish silliness'.

PLATE 23: MIDDLESEX

The small size of Middlesex has allowed the cartographer more space for topographic detail – bridges, parks, the windmill on the

Hampstead heights, the church on Harrow Hill. Seen from such hill-tops the country appeared 'like a Paradise and Garden of God', studded with fine country mansions. Within easy ride of London were 'Five princely Houses, and many other Houses of the Nobility, Knights and Gentlemen, and also of the worthy Citizens of London, so sumptuously built and pleasantly situated as the like is not to be found anywhere'. Nearness to London also benefited lesser folk. The farmer's wife (Norden relates) 'or twice or thrice a weeke conveyeth to London mylke, butter, cheese, apples, pears, frumentye, hennes, chickens, egges, baken and a thousand other country drugges'. Leland's ride back to London through Middlesex took him through Uxbridge, then a single long street of timber houses, many of them inns, and 'from Uxbridge to Southall, a village, about 6 Miles. Thence to Acton, a pretty Thorough-fare, a 4 Miles. Thence to Mariburne Brook and Park a 4 Miles. This Brooke runneth by the Parke-Wall of St James to London a 2 Miles.' As to London, 'her wealth grows from the revenues and harvest of her South-bounding Thames', and Camden saw her as the 'epitome of all Britain, the seat of the British Empire'. With perhaps a quarter of a million inhabitants, London had no rival.

PLATE 24: NORFOLK

There was great variety in this large and rich county: 'the soil in some parts is fat, luscious and moist, as in Marshland and Flegg: in others, especially to the west, it is poor, lean and sandy; and in others chalky. But the goodness of the soil may be gathered from hence, that the inhabitants are of a bright, clear complexion; not to mention their sharpness of wit, and singular capacity for the study of our common law.' Sharpness of wit, of course, is as you find it, and 'Norfolk full of wiles' was a very old saying. The city of Norwich had produced many famous men and was remarkably beautiful. Camden doubted whether to call it a City in an Orchard or an Orchard in a City, 'so equally are houses and trees blended'.

PLATE 25: NORTHAMPTONSHIRE

This fertile and favourite shire 'everywhere adorned with noblemen's and gentlemen's houses and very full of towns and churches' (thirty might be counted from a single viewpoint, and many more wind-mills) prided itself on maintaining all its population on the land. It had no need of industry, then regarded simply as a means of relieving poor landless cottagers. Here stood Holdenby House, built by Sir Christopher Hatton (so he said) 'for the greatest and last monument of his youth', a youth he did not long survive. The mansion, too, has gone. Further east, perched high above the Nene, stood Fotheringay Castle, beautified within by Catherine of Aragon, and later the home of another tragic queen. Even the loyal Camden could hardly forgive Elizabeth for her execution of the lovely Mary. 'Let it be for ever forgotten [he said]. Even the best princes are sometimes violently hurried away, as good pilots by tempests, whither they would not.'

PLATE 26: NORTHUMBERLAND

This county, full (as the map shows) of castles raised against the moss-troopers, was for the most part rough and barren. Its harshness 'seems to have hardened the very carcasses of the inhabitants [exclaims Camden]; whom the neighbouring Scots have rendered yet more hardy, sometimes inuring them to war, and sometimes amicably communicating their customs and way of living: whence they have become a most warlike people and excellent horsemen. There is not a man of fashion among them but has his little castle and fort.' At the crossing of the Tyne stood Newcastle, the richest of all the towns in this county, for of it the poet wrote:

> Why seek ye fire of some exalted sphere?
> Earth's fruitful bosom will supply you here.

Its wealthy coal-masters were no warriors, and the city owed its walls to one of them who was carried off and held to ransom by the Scots in the days of Edward I. The sum was paid, and, on the prisoner's return, he invoked the aid of his fellow-citizens and set about making his home town secure.

PLATE 27: NOTTINGHAMSHIRE

Running through the heart of the shire is the Vale of Trent, rich in corn and cattle, upon which Nottingham City looks down, 'standing stately on its clyning hill'. Sherwood Forest covered the great belt of poor sandy soil west of the Trent, and of boastful people it used to be said in Nottingham, 'Many talk of Robin Hood who never shot in his bow'. Much of the Forest had given way to tillage by Tudor days, and it sheltered Newstead Abbey, the seat of Lord Byron's forebears. 'Sherwood my fuel, Trent my fish supplies', Nottinghamshire folk used to say, but in fact, as Camden tells us, 'many of them burn pit-coal, the smell whereof is very offensive'.

PLATE 28: OXFORDSHIRE

'The Aire milde, temperate and delicate; the land fertile, pleasant and bounteous; in a word both Heaven and Earth accord to make the Inhabitants healthful and happy.' And in their midst is 'seated on a rising vale the most famous University of Oxford, our most noble Athens, the seat of our English Muses, the prop and the pillar, nay the sun, the eye and the very soul of the nation, whence religion, letters and good manners are plentifully diffused through the whole kingdom'. Camden, who wrote this, was himself an Oxford man. Yet good manners, at least, do not seem to have been diffused to all parts even of Oxfordshire: for to any uncouth, rustical sort of fellow the Elizabethans used to say 'You were born at Hog's Norton' – the Hoke-Norton of our map.

PLATE 29: RUTLANDSHIRE

With so small a county to fill his page the draughtsman could use a scale admitting of minor topographical detail. He puts in, for example, the Beacon Hill, near Moorcot, the Boundary Stone, near Belmisthorpe; the two bridges at Stamford and Casterton that carried the Great North Road towards York. As to the origin of this little Shire, the legend ran that 'one Rutter, a Man of great Favor with his Prince, that desired to have of Reward of hym as much land as he could ride over in a day on a Horse of Woode, rid over as much as is now Rutlandshire by Arte Magick, and he was after swallowed into the Yerth'.

PLATE 30: SHROPSHIRE

The Welsh mountains thrust out long fingers into Shropshire – Breidden Hill, the Stiper Stones, Brown Clee – and across the Severn the solitary Wrekin. To keep the Welsh within bounds, a wall of castles, some thirty-two in this county alone, was erected: Clun Castle, held by the Fitz-Alans; Ludlow Castle, built by Roger de Montgomery; New Castle, Hopton Castle, and Bishop's Castle, kept by the Bishop of Hereford. 'Sabrina fair', the Severn flowing through the midst of the Shire, almost encompasses Shrewsbury.

PLATE 31: SOMERSETSHIRE

This 'large and plentiful county', as Camden terms it, was 'on every side garnished with Pastures and delightful Meadows, and beautified with Manor houses, both many and faire'. In fact, it was a dairy county, famous for Cheddar cheese. But although it had everything 'to content the purse, the heart, the eye', there was a local proverb saying: 'What is best for the Abider is worst for the Rider'. For the heavy, fat and fruitful soils were so foul and miry in winter that travel was attended by great difficulty. Two famous cities attracted strangers. Bristol, adopted home of John Cabot, and famous for its unique underground sewers removing 'all noysome filth and uncleanness', was a city of merchants. Bath, a few miles away, was a city of healing. Yet although piped water was laid on to the houses, the conditions in the hot baths were incredibly sordid.

PLATE 32: STAFFORDSHIRE

The hills and moors of North Staffordshire, where the wind blows cold and the snow lies long on the ground, were no friends to tillage. But they gave birth to clear streams like the Dove of which it was said 'In April Dove's flood, Is worth a King's good': for the water enriched the lush meadows about Uttoxeter, esteemed the best grazing in all England. Not far away was Needwood Forest, graced with many parks 'wherein the gentry hereabouts frequently exercise themselves with great application, in the agreeable toil of hunting'. But conditions were very different in the south of the county, where round about Walsall and Wolverhampton miners worked iron and pit-coal. 'But whether to their loss or advantage [says Camden] the natives themselves are the best judges, and to them I refer it.'

PLATE 33: SUFFOLK

The 'fair maids of Suffolk' were proverbial for their looks, owing their roses perhaps to the climate, said to be the best in the world, or to the rich cream which they also made into cheese. Suffolk cheeses, huge and satisfying, were esteemed as far away as Spain, as well as by Cambridge undergraduates, and as standard provision for English ships. The county lies off the beaten track and strange things were said to happen there. 'In the hearte of the Shire two greene boyes of Satyres kind arose out of the ground from the Antipodes – believe it if you will', says Camden.

PLATE 34: SURREY

'The aire in this Shire is most sweet and delectable, so that for the same cause many royall Palaces of our Princes are there seated.' They included Non-such, Oatlands and Richmond, where Queen

Elizabeth herself 'having glutted Nature with length of days, was received into the heavenly choir'. At Effingham the Lord High Admiral, Lord Howard, victor over the Armada, had his seat. The wonder of the county was the burrowing Mole, for the river of that name (which sinks into the chalk) was believed to seek a passage underground to avoid the opposition of the Downs, and the cartographer duly pricks its hidden course upon the map.

PLATE 35: SUSSEX

'Sussex full of dirt and mire' said the proverb, for every traveller on his way to Rye or Chichester had to cross the vale of sticky clay between the sandy Forest Ridges and the chalky South Downs. Besides its wealth of corn and grass and sheep, Sussex had notable industries of iron and glass, looked at somewhat askance, however, 'for as they bring great gain to their possessors, so they impoverish the country of wood, whose want will be found in ages to come, if not at this present in some sort felt'. A prophecy amply fulfilled.

PLATE 36: WARWICKSHIRE

The river Avon parted this shire into two regions, the Feldon and the Woodland – the former an open or 'champain' country whose fertile fields of corn and verdant pastures delighted the eye and yielded a most pleasant prospect to a farming nation, the latter the ancient forest of Arden, haunt of robbers and red deer. In Elizabethan days it had been deeply encroached upon by towns and villages and its great trees thinned to feed the blow-furnaces of iron-smelters. But the landscape, rich in trees and woods, still deserved its name. At Stratford-on-Avon men did not yet pride themselves upon Shakespeare, they preferred to remember Hugh Clopton, Lord Mayor of London, who had presented his native town with a 'sumptuous bridge' of stone, spanning the river and flood-meadows in fourteen arches. Warwick and Coventry were Warwickshire's most famous cities, the latter struggling against the change of fashion which had destroyed the market for men's caps dyed 'Coventry true blue'. But Birmingham was beginning to forge ahead, already 'swarming with inhabitants', and echoing with the ring of anvils.

PLATE 8: WESTMORLAND

The new-fashioned style of country house was not to be seen up in the north. Buildings were plain and strong, as in Cumberland, 'generally built castle-wise for defence of themselves, their tenants and their goods, whenever the Scots should make their inroads'. And Westmorland was poor: Appleby in the pretty Eden Valley little more than a village, although the county town. Kendal was more prosperous, for its cloth industry, based on the soft-woolled mountain sheep, was famous throughout England.

PLATE 37: WILTSHIRE

In this county 'fair and plain' still stands one of the ancient Wonders of Britain, *Gigantum Chorea,* as the Elizabethans called it, the Giant's Dance, Stonehenge. 'It is unaccountable [declares Camden] how such stones should come there, seeing all that country wants ordinary stones for building, and by what means they were raised.' Six miles away the lovely cathedral of Salisbury 'with its high steeple and double cross-aisles, by a venerable kind of grandeur strikes the spectator with a sacred joy and admiration'. The city itself, adorned with 'sumptuous and delicate buildings', was kept sweet and clean, like Winchester, by rivulets derived from a clear chalk stream and led through every street.

PLATE 38: WORCESTERSHIRE

Its fields, hedgerows and highways 'beset with useful pear-trees', its rich vales of Severn and Evesham full of corn, and adjacent to them the ancient Forests of Wyre and Feckenham, the great woods of

Norton and lovely Malvern Chace, Worcestershire lacked for nothing in Tudor eyes. The Severn 'with slow course and as it were admiring, passeth by Worcester, seated on its bank. And it really deserves admiration, both for its antiquity and its beauty. But its great glory consists in its inhabitants, who are numerous, courteous, and wealthy by means of the clothing trade.'

PLATE 39: YORKSHIRE

The largest English county does not lack variety. 'If in one place it be of a stony, sandy nature, in another it is pregnant and fruitful: and so, if it be naked and exposed in one part, we find it cloathed and sheltered with great store of wood in another: Nature using an alloy and mixture, that the entire county by their variety might appear more pleasing and beautiful.' In the West Riding, Sheffield 'among other little towns hereabouts' had even before Chaucer's day become remarkable for its smiths and edge-tools. Halifax was becoming known for its new clothing trade. 'Which confirms the truth of that old observation [says Camden] that a barren country is a great whet to the industry of the natives.' In the East Riding the decay of Hedon and the rise of brick-built Hull (enriched by the Iceland trade) proved that 'the condition of towns and cities is every jot as unstable as that of men'. Above the vales of the North Riding the moorlands rose 'black and mountainous, rugged and unsightly, by reason of crags, hills and woods'. Where the Ridings met stood York, the second city of England.

PLATE 40: WALES AND MONMOUTHSHIRE

The English castles planted strategically throughout Wales had for the most part been left to decay before Leland's day. For few would wish to dwell in these wild parts, with their forbidding mountains, a region where even the gentry were men of 'but mean estate' in English eyes. Leland's judgment was harsh. The Welsh (he said) 'dyd

study more to Pasturage than Tylling, as Favourers of Their con-
suete idleness'. And it was true that they could turn out cattle, sheep, ponies and goats without stint on the natural hill-pastures while still leaving grazing for the red deer and conies. But change was at hand. Sea-coal was already dug in the south, near Kidwelly, and in the north in Flintshire. England was demanding Welsh wool and coarse friezes. Here, too, the shadow of Industrial Revolution crept forward over the countryside.

Thanks are due to Mr R. A. Skelton and the staff of the Map Room at the British Museum for their kindly help in the preparation of this book

THE KINGDOME OF ENGLAND
Part of Scotland
Part of Ireland
The German Ocean
The Irish Sea
Isle of Man
Anglesey
Wight
The Scale of Miles
Barwick
Warkworth C.
Bottel C.
Newcastle
Carlisle
Hexham
Durasme
Wilton
Whitby
Kilham
York
Hul
Waxham
Grimsby
Sutton
Lyncolne
Burnham
Nortwich
Lyn
Dowham
Yarmouth
Waldersw.yk
Thetford
Cambridg
Ipswiche
Huntington
Colchester
Malden
Canterbury
Dover
Rochester
London
Oxford
Bedford
Warwik
Coventre
Nottingam
Lecester
Peterbu
Darby
Stafford
Mannsfeld
Chester
Manchester
Lancaster
Settle
Ripley
Kendal
Egremont
Darlington
Wirkinton
Millum
Ulverston
Kirkham
Denbigh
Bangor
Shrowesbur
Montgomery
Dolgelle
Machenlet
Cardigan
Bealt
Hereford
Monmouth
Carmarthin
Llangadok
S. Davids
Penbrok
Glocester
Barkley
Brystol
Bathe
Reding
Winsor
Rigate
Salesburi
Welles
Winchester
Southampton
Chechester
Newport
Dorcester
Exceter
Morton
Bedford
Dunster
Ilfracombe
Stratton
Padstow
The Landes end
Sorlings
7. Stones
Plymmouth
Portlandt
Penard C.
S. Donets
Rushin C.
Carlisle
Garleis
Anan
Knok fergus
Arglas
Dundalek
Drogdagh
Dublin
Caryek
Waterford
Newbury
Newin
Texel
Alcmaer
Egmont
Leyden
Zierixzee
Middelburg
Ghenast
Antwerpen
Grevelinge
Cales
45
90

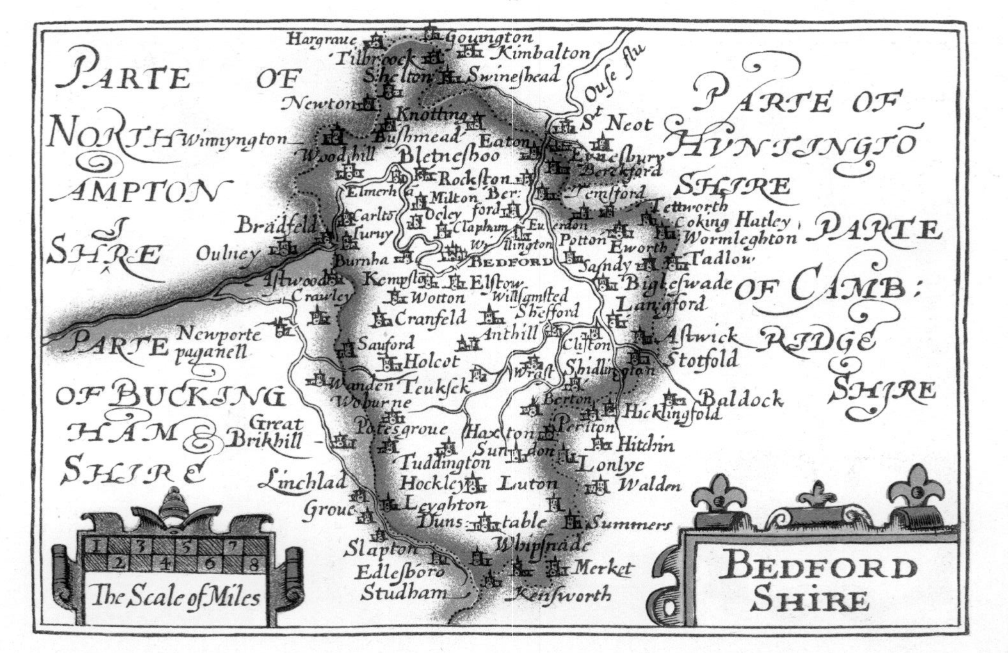
Bedford Shire
The Scale of Miles
1 2 3 4 5 6 7 8
Parte of Northampton Shire
Parte of Huntington Shire
Parte of Camb: ridge Shire
Parte of Buckingham Shire
Ouse flu
Hargraue
Goungton
Kimbalton
Tilbroock
Shelton
Swineshead
Newton
Knotting
Wimyngton
Bushmead
Eaton
St Neot
Woodhill
Bletneshoo
Eynesbury
Berckford
Rockston
Temsford
Elmerh
Milton
Ber: ford
Carlto
Ocley
Tettworth
Bradfeld
Clapham
Euerdon
Coking Hatley
Wormleghton
Surny
Potton
Eworth
Oulney
Burnha
Bedford
Sandy
Tadlow
Astwood
Kempston
Elstow
Bigleswade
Crawley
Wotton
Willsamsted
Langford
Cranfeld
Shefford
Newporte paganell
Astwick
Anthill
Sauford
Clifton
Stotfold
Holcot
Shidlington
Wrast
Wanden
Teuksek
Woborne
Berton
Baldock
Hicklingfold
Great Brikhill
Potesgroue
Haxton
Periton
Sundon
Hitchin
Tuddington
Lonlye
Hockley
Luton
Walden
Linchlad
Leyghton
Groue
Duns:table
Summers
Slapton
Whipsnade
Edlesboro
Merket
Studham
Kensworth

BARK:
SHIRE
1 2 3 4 5 6 7 8 9 10
The Scale of Miles
PARTE OF BUCKING: HAM SHIRE
PARTE OF OX: FORD SHIRE
PARTE OF WILT SHIRE
PARTE OF HAM SHIRE
PARTE OF SURREY
Oxford
Witham
Sanford
Witne
Kennington
Abington
Longworth
Hinton
Gratton
Kenscot
Nuneaton
Cliston
Dorchester
Hurley
Grene land
Marcha
Garford
Lach lad
Farringdo
Colleshul
Pusay
Chilrey
Draton
Sutton
Locking
Hagthorn
Wallingford
Henley
Madenhead
Colbrock
Windsor
Kingston
Coton
Wantage
Bulbery
Aston
Chaulsey
Goring
Sunning
Bisham
Braye
Twifort
Hurst
Cluworth
Binfeld
Warfeld
Stanes
Hyworth
Scriuenham
Iyle
Farinborow
Stretley
Kingsletcob
Albury
Cumpton
Lamborn
East Isley
Stanford
Litle
Shelford
Yattington
Reading
Purley
Great Shelford
Boxford
Winterhorne
Sutham
Okingham
Wingfeld
Chilton
Welford
Demiston
Bucklesbury
Arberfeld
Easthampsted
Shan
Thatsham
Oston
Blukha
Sandherst
Rainsbury
Wickham
Aldermersto
Hungerford
Nuberye
Wasing
Swallofeld
Newto

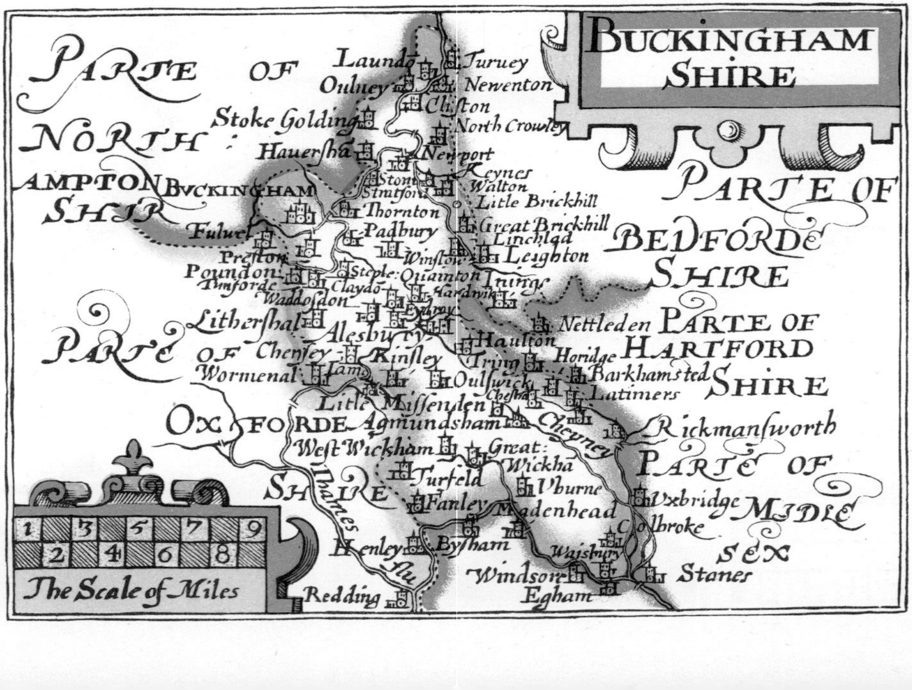

BUCKINGHAM SHIRE
PARTE OF NORTH: AMPTON SHIR
PARTE OF BEDFORDE SHIRE
PARTE OF HARTFORD SHIRE
PARTE OF MIDLE SEX
PARTE OF OXFORDE SHIRE
Laundo
Turuey
Oulney
Neweton
Clifton
Stoke Golding
North Crowley
Hauersha
Newport
Keynes
Walton
Stone
Stratford
Litle Brickhill
BUCKINGHAM
Thornton
Great Brickhill
Linchlad
Fulwel
Padbury
Leighton
Preston
Winslow
Poundon
Steple:
Quainton
Trings
Tinforde
Claydo
Hardwik
Waddosdon
Eythrop
Nettleden
Lithershal
Alesbury
Haulton
Chensey
Kinsley
Tring
Horidge
Wormenal
Tame
Oulswick
Barkhamsted
Chesham
Latimers
Litle Missenden
Agmundsham
Cheyney
Rickmansworth
West Wickham
Great: Wickha
Turfeld
Vburne
Thames
Fanley
Madenhead
Uxbridge
Colbroke
Henley
Bysham
Waisbury
Flu
Windsor
Staines
Egham
Redding
1 2 3 4 5 6 7 8 9
The Scale of Miles

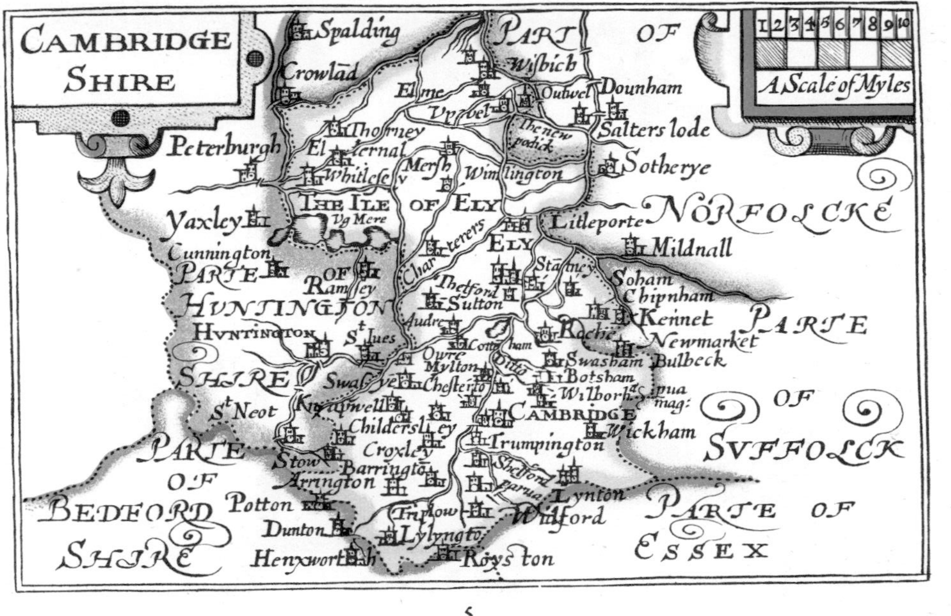
CAMBRIDGE SHIRE
A Scale of Myles
1 2 3 4 5 6 7 8 9 10
Spalding
Crowlād
Peterburgh
Yaxley
Cunnington
PARTE OF HUNTINGTON SHIRE
Huntington
Ramsey
St Iues
St Neot
THE ILE OF ELY
Vg Mere
Thorney
Whitlesey
Elme
Wisbich
Outwel
Dounham
Salters lode
Sotherye
The new podick
Wimlington
Litleporte
NORFOLCKE
Mildnall
Charterers
ELY
Thetford
Sulton
Soham
Chipnham
Kennet
Newmarket
Bulbeck
Cottenham
Swasham
Botsham
CAMBRIDGE
Wickham
Trumpington
Croxley
Barrington
Arrington
Stow
Potton
Dunton
Henxworth
Royston
Lynton
PARTE OF SUFFOLCK
PARTE OF ESSEX
PARTE OF BEDFORD SHIRE

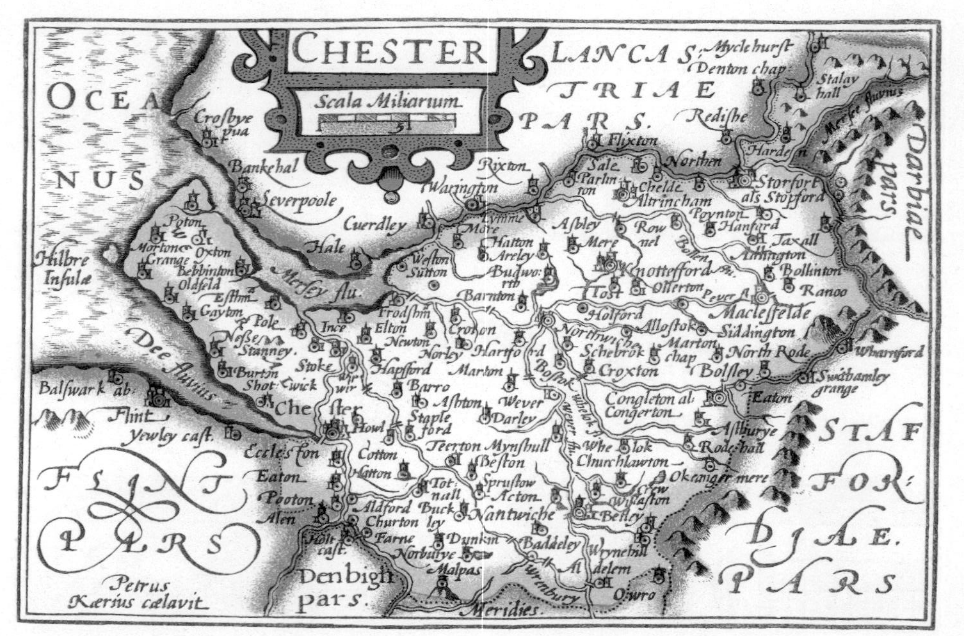
CHESTER
Scala Miliarium
OCEANUS
LANCASTRIAE PARS.
Darbiae pars
STAFFORDIAE PARS
FLINT PARS
Denbigh pars.
Meridies.
Hilbre Insulæ
Dee fluvius
Mersey flu.
Merse fluvius
Crosbye pua
Bankehal
Severpoole
Cuerdley
Hale
Waringtton
Rixton
Flixton
Sale
Parlinton
Chelde
Altrincham
Northen
Redishe
Myclehurst
Denton chap
Stalay hall
Harden
Storfort als Stopford
Poynton
Hanford
Taxall
Bollinton
Ranoo
Maclesfelde
Siddington
North Rode
Wharnford
Swithamley grange
Bolsley
Eaton
Congleton al: Congerton
Asburye
Rodehall
Okeanger mere
Churchlawton
Crew
Wistaston
Betley
Wynehill
Aldelem
Owro
Wrenbury
Baddeley
Malpas
Norburye
Dunkin
Farne
Churton
Holt cast.
Aldford
Buckley
Nantwiche
Acton
Sprustow
Beston
Tottnall
Hatton
Cotton
Eccleston
Eaton
Pooton
Alen
Chester
Howl
Stapleford
Ashton
Wever
Darley
Teerton
Mynshull
Barro
Hapsford
Marton
Norley
Hartford
Newton
Elton
Frodshm
Ince
Stoke
Wirwir
Croton
Barnton
Budworth
Arley
Hatton
More
Lymme
Weston
Sutton
Asbley
Mere
Rownel
Knottesford
Tost
Ollerton
Holford
Allostok
Northwiche
Schebrok
Croxton
Marton chap
Bostok
Whelok
Poton
Morton Grange
Oxton
Bebbinton
Oldfeld
Esthm
Gayton
Pole
Nesse
Stanney
Burton
Shotwick
Balswark ab.
Flint
Yewley cast.
Petrus Kærius cælavit

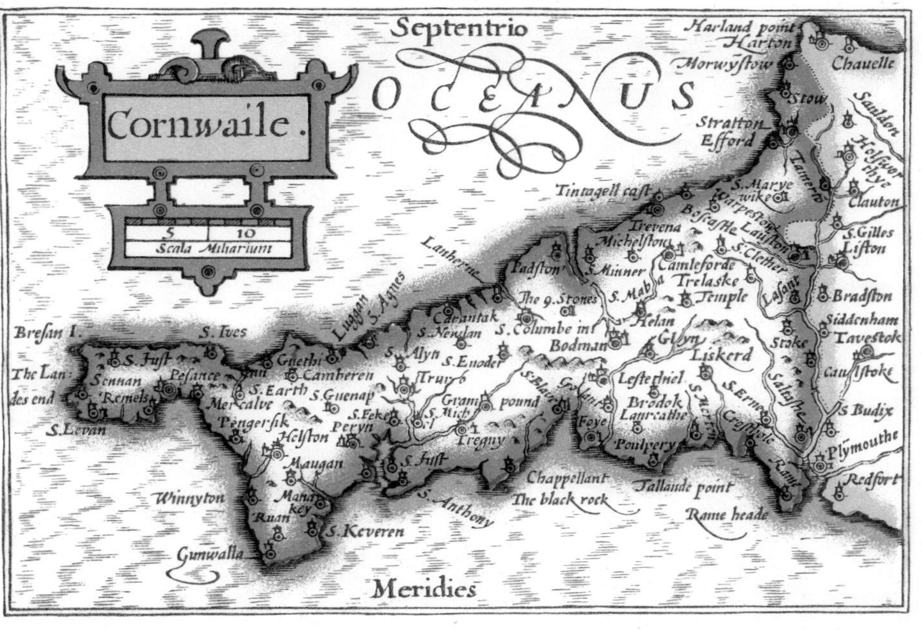
Cornwaile.
Scala Miliarium
5
10
Septentrio
OCEANUS
Meridies
Bresan I.
The Landes end
Sennan
Remels
S. Just
S. Levan
S. Ives
Pesance
Mercalve
S. Earth
Guethi
Camberen
S. Guenap
Pengersik
Helston
Peryn
S. Feke
Maugan
Winnyton
Manakey
Ruan
Gunwalla
S. Keveren
Luggan
S. Agnes
Lanherne
Carantak
S. Newlan
S. Alyn
S. Enoder
Truro
Gram pound
S. Mich
Tregny
S. Just
S. Anthony
Padston
The 9. Stones
S. Columbe int
Bodman
Chappellant
The black rock
Foye
Poulpery
Lestethiel
Brodok
Laurcathe
Tallande point
Rame heade
Tintagell cast
Trevena
Michelstow
S. Minner
S. Mab
Helan
Glyn
Camleforde
Trelaske
Temple
Liskerd
S. Erne
Crofthole
Rame
Boscastle
Warpestow
S. Marye wike
Launston
S. Clether
Lasant
Stake
Saltashe
Plymouthe
Redfort
Harland point
Harton
Morwystow
Stow
Stratton
Efford
Lamerto
Chauelle
Sauldon
Holsworthye
Clauton
S. Gilles
Lifton
Bradston
Siddenham
Tavestok
Caulstoke
S Budix

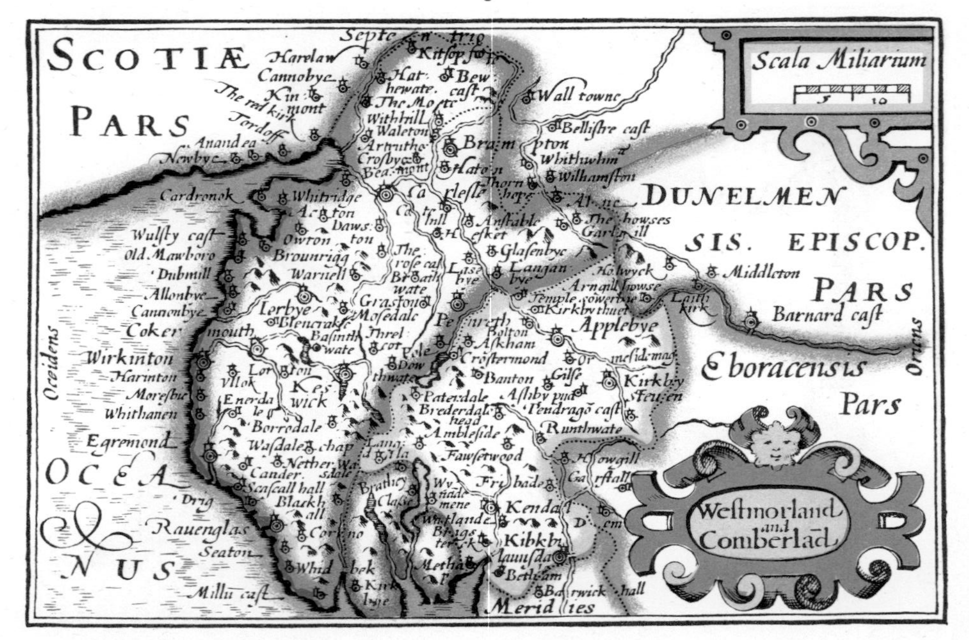
Westmorland and Comberlad
Scala Miliarium
SCOTIÆ PARS
DUNELMENSIS. EPISCOP. PARS
Eboracensis Pars
OCEANUS
Septentrio
Meridies
Occidens
Oriens
Harelaw
Cannobye
Kinmont
The red kirk
Tordoff
Anandea
Newbye
Kitsop
Bewcast
Wall towne
Bellistre cast
Brampton
Whithwhm
Wilhamston
Carlesle
Cardronok
Whitridge
Wulsty cast
Old Mawboro
Dubmill
Allonbye
Cannonbye
Cokermouth
Wirkinton
Harinton
Moresbie
Whithauen
Egremond
Drig
Rauenglas
Seaton
Millu cast
Brounrigg
Warnell
Lerbye
Blencrake
Kes wick
Borrodale
Wasdale chap
Nether Wasdale
Cander
Scascall hall
Blackhall
Whid bek
Kirk
Glasenbye
Langan bye
Penreth
Askham
Crostermond
Applebye
Kirkby Steuen
Banton
Paterdale
Brederdale head
Ambleside
Runthwate
Fawsetwood
Kendal
Kibkby lauusdal
Bethlam
Barwick hall
Howgill
Garsfall
Middleton
Barnard cast
Laith kirk
Arngill howse
Temple sowerbie
Kirkbythuer
Gilse
Ashby pud
Peudragō cast
Brathey
Clase
Metha
Graston
Mosedale
Threlcot
Dowthwate
Basinthwate
Enerdale
Lorton
Vllok

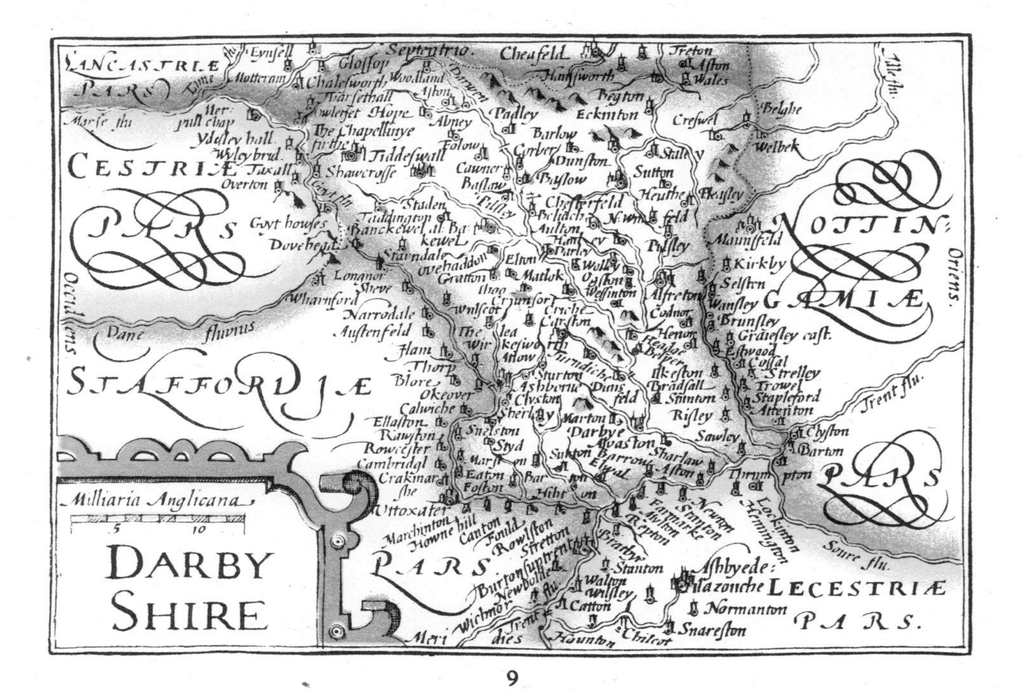
DARBY
SHIRE
Milliaria Anglicana
5
10
Septentrio.
Oriens.
Occidens.
LANCASTRIÆ PARS
CESTRIÆ PARS
STAFFORDIÆ PARS
NOTTINGAMIÆ PARS
LECESTRIÆ PARS.
Dane fluvius
Trent flu.
Soure flu.
Idle flu.
Glossop
Chealesworth
Woodland
Chesfeld
Hansworth
Beyton
Eckinton
Treton
Aston
Wales
Creswel
Belghe
Welbek
Padley
Barlow
Dunston
Baslow
Stalley
Sutton
Heuthe
Chesterfeld
Tiddeswall
Shawcrosse
Hope
Abney
Folow
Staden
Taddington
Banckewel al: Bakewel
Dovehead
Gyt howses
Taxall
Overton
Starndale
Longnor
Shene
Wharnford
Elton
Matlok
Gratton
Wolley
Ogston
Wessinton
Alfreton
Pinsley
Maunsfeld
Kirkby
Selston
Wansley
Brunsley
Gräiesley cast.
Eswood
Cossal
Strelley
Trowel
Stapleford
Attenton
Codnor
Henor
Ilkeston
Bradsall
Stanton
Risley
Sawley
Clyston
Barton
Thrumpton
Lockinton
Hemington
Narrodale
Austenfeld
Flam
Thorp
Blore
Okeover
Calwiche
Ellaston
Rawston
Rowcester
Cambridgl
Crakmarshe
Uttoxater
Ashborne
Clyston
Sherley
Snelston
Styd
Marston
Darbye
Aloaston
Sharlaw
Aston
Barrow
Elwal
Sutton
Eaton
Foston
Hilton
Marchinton
Howne hill
Canton
Rowlston
Stretton
Burton super trent
Newbolle
Repton
Newton
Stanton
Farmarke
Milton
Bradby
Stanton
Walton
Ashbyede la zouche
Normanton
Snareston
Catton
Chilcot
Wichmor
Meri

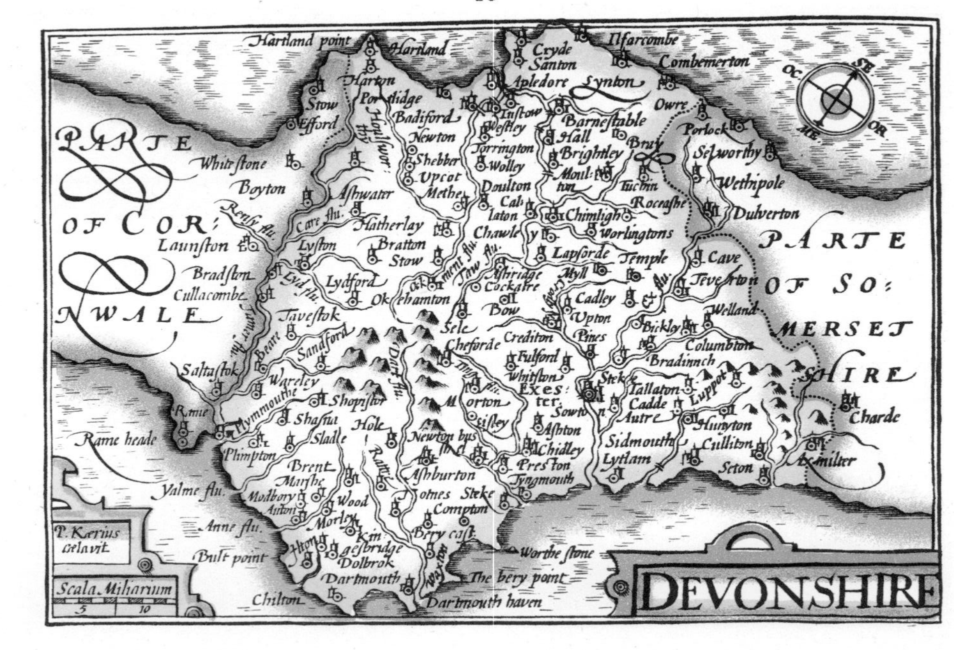
DEVONSHIRE
PARTE OF CORNWALE
PARTE OF SOMERSET SHIRE
P. Kerius cælavit
Scala Miliarium
5
10
Hartland point
Harland
Harton
Stow
Efford
Whitstone
Boyton
Launston
Bradston
Cullacombe
Saltastok
Rame
Rame heade
Yalme flu.
Anne flu.
Bult point
Chilton
Porthidge
Houlsworthy
Badiford
Newton
Shebber
Upcot
Methe
Ashwater
Hatherlay
Bratton
Stow
Lyston
Lydford
Okehamton
Tavestok
Sandford
Wareley
Plymmouthe
Shopistor
Shastu
Sladle
Hole
Plimpton
Brent
Marshe
Modbory
Auton
Wood
Morley
Kingesbridge
Dolbrok
Dartmouth
Dartmouth haven
The bery point
Worthe stone
Bery cast.
Compton
Steke
Totnes
Ashburton
Newton bushel
Dart flu.
Cryde
Santon
Apledore
Synton
Ilfarcombe
Combemerton
Owre
Porlock
Selworthy
Wethpole
Dulverton
Instow
Westley
Torrington
Wolley
Doulton
Callaton
Chawley
Barnestable
Hall
Brightley
Moulton
Tuchin
Rocrashe
Bray
Chimligh
Worlingtons
Lapsorde
Temple
Myll
Cave
Teverton
Ashridge
Cockatre
Bow
Sele
Cheforde
Crediton
Cadley
Upton
Pines
Welland
Bickley
Columbton
Bradinnch
Fulford
Whitston
Exester
Morton
Sisley
Ashton
Chidley
Preston
Tyngmouth
Steke
Tallaton
Cadde
Autre
Luppot
Hunyton
Culliton
Sidmouth
Lytlam
Seton
Charde
Axmilter
Taw flu.
Lyd flu.
Care flu.
Tamer flu.

Dorcet Shire
The Scale of miles
5
10
Petrus Kærius cælavit.
Septentrio.
Occidens.
Oriens.
Meridies.
PART OF WILT SHIRE
PARTE OF SOMERSET SHIRE.
OCEANUS
Mere
Pen
Stoke
Wynecaunton
Gillinghm
Sylton
Ham
Bugley
Stoure
Safesbury
Can
Crafonde
Fiseltude
Tudboro
Marnhul
Sutton
Craneborne
Weke
Yenstone
Corton
Sherbor cast:
Stalbridge
Blakemo
Evill
Berwick
Clausworth
Charde
Suttonbinghm
Wynsfhm
Mysterton
Clapton
Ryme
Hilsfeld
Melbury bub
Pullam
Hasilbere
Foke
Stoke
Sturmister newton cast:
Ibberton
Blandford
Stepleton
Boreson
Knolton
Horton
Holte
Hinton
Worthe
Wet: wood
Ring wood
Set: Christchurche
Launston
Wimborn mynster
Tarrant
Ruston
Stickland
Middleton
Carleton
Spesbury
Clenston
Corfe
Lake
Holenest
Tomson
Hamworthy
Poole
Maypoider
Phische
Piddlehinton
Cerneab:
Forston
Frampton
Aspudle
Burston
Muston
Bere
Holton
Kesmorthe
Hyde
Warehm
Anen
Slepe
Stowboro
Owre
Corfe Castel
Bradle
Steple
Stoke
Wool
Morten
Owre
Dorchester
Upwey
Sutton
Ryngston
Sandesfoote castel
Weke
Portland castel
Flete
Langton
Baldon
Swyre
Lytton
Sout hover
Byrton
Burport
Frome
Mitton
Hoke
Forde
Bemyster
Pamnhm
Axmyster
Simmesboro
Lyme
Uplyme
Cullyton
Axmouth
Beane
Mem bym
Whitstanton

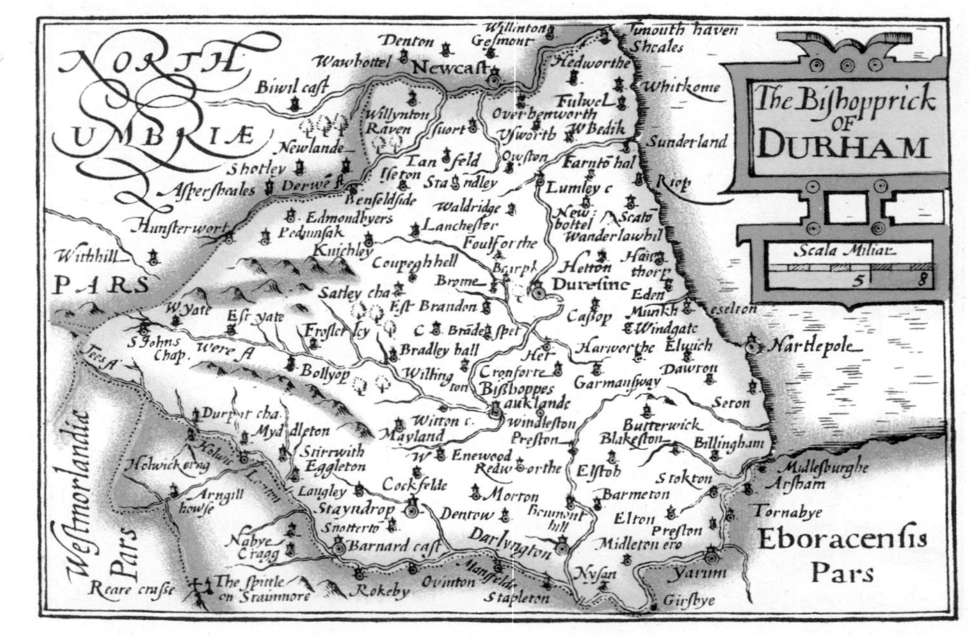
The Bishopprick OF DURHAM
Scala Miliar
5
8
NORTH UMBRIÆ PARS
Westmorlandia Pars
Eboracensis Pars
Newcast
Duresme
Sunderland
Hartlepole
Darlyngton
Barnard cast
Stokton
Yarum
Tynmouth haven
Shcales
Whitkome
Bishoppes aukland
Staindrop
Lanchester
Lumley c
Billingham
Midlesburghe

ESSEX COVNTY
Scala Miliarum
5
10
Septentrio
Occidens
OCEANUS
Parte of Cambridge
Parte of Hartforde
Parte of Suffolke
Royston
Haidon
Linton
Hempstede
Walden
Thaxted
Finchingfeld
Halsted
Bocking
Coggeshall
Colchester
Ipswiche
Nacton
Walton
Branthm
Shotley
Manitre
Harwich
Tendringe
Frating
Holland
Wiston
Lammarshe
Yeldam magna
Whit colne
Erles colne
Shawford
Bray ntre
Eastre ford
Ferring
Peldon
Tolesbury
Langford
Maldon
Bradwell
Norton
Dengie
Crikesey
Foulnesse
Shoburye
Hawkeswell
S. Fambrige
Stock
Widford
Belericay
Langdon
Brentwoode
Rumford
Chigwell
Woodforde
Layton
Barkinge
Muckinge
Coringham
Thurrock gray
Grauesend
Grane
Warden
Shepye Insula
Tamesis fluvius
London
Blackwall
Dert ford
Grynwiche
Chelmes forde
Willingales
Engerston
Keluedon
Waltham crucis
Epping strete
Hoddesdon
Chingford
Newiton
Lauer
Hadfeld brodcoke
Prashe
Felsted
Firested
Waltham p.
Boreham
Sherringe
Bisshopster ford
Barkwey
Clauering
Tyltey
Easton p.
Dunmow
Ware
Hasling
Burbrock
Clare
Henny
Sudbury
Tilburye
Stamborne
Hanerill

Glocester Shire
Vigorniæ pars
Bytford
Evesholme
Quenton
Pershore
Elmely
Wikeford
Hynton
Campden
PARS OXONII
Lydbury
Bekford
Bradwey
Didbrok
Longborow
Tewkesbury
Wulston
Winchcombe
Stow on the would
Preston
Pantley
Newent
The Lye
Cheltenham
Minsterworth
Whittenton
Idbury
Gotheridge Cast
Huntley
Coberley
N. Leche
Burford
Dean
Glocester
Newinham
Hascombe
Biburye
Esllechc
Munmouth
Pennale
Chierwal
Wynston
Stronde
Lechlande
MONUMETHENSIS PARS
Blackeney
Saperton
Cirencester al. Ciciter
Erampton
Minchinhampton
Barekley
BERCERIAE PARS
Avington
Dursley
Tetbury
Crekelade
Wolton
Cheptow
Thornbury
Weckewar
WILTONIÆ PARS
Littleton
Badmanton
Aunsburye
Chippm. sodeburye
Bristol
Hambrock
Wraxhal
Marsvelde
Croc hampill
Mil. Ang
5
10
15

SOUT: HAMPTON.
Sala Miliarum
5
10
Occidens
Oriens
PARTE OF WILSHIRE
PARTE OF DORSETSHIRE
PARTE OF SOUTH SEX
OCEANUS
WIGHT INS
Hunger: ford
Newbrry
Swalofelt
Sandherst
Erymley
Inkepen
Tadolowe
Yateley
Newtowne
Kingelcliere
Hertleywesport
Combes
Croukeaston
Basingstoke
Aldershare
Gylford
Lynkenholt
Lauerstoke
Ashe
Odiam
South
Fernhm
Hursbornetarrant
Dummur
Godal
Lurgisala
Steuenton
Bradley
Aulton
Elsted
myngе
Andouer
Hedley
Shipton
Fullingtot
Est Straton
Maydstede
Okehanger
Quarley
Grethm
Stockbridge
Ripley
Hackley
Longstoke
Winchester
Easton
Ovington
Alresford
Froxfeld
Petersfelde
Sarum
Motterstunt
Twiforde
Bisshops walthum
West Meane
Clanfe
Nusted
Midherste
Otterborton
E Dean
Stanbridge
Rumsey
Bishopstoke
Caterington
Beriton
Chilton
Dunckton
Hale
Southhumton
Nerleycast
Sutwick
Hauant
Farum
Chichestra
Rockborn
Eling
Hokes
Alderstoke
Harbradge
Ellingham
Cranborne
Leape
Exburie
S. Andros
Chelsey
West Wetering
Reugwood
Boldere
Calshot cast
Portesmouth
Bisthorne
Auen
Lemyngton
Christchurche
Holeness
Hurst cast

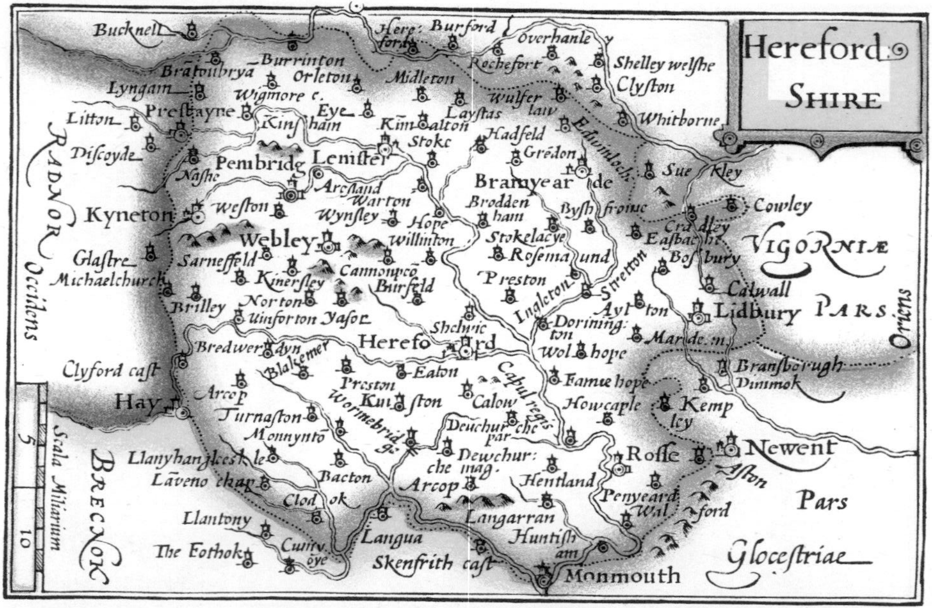
Hereford SHIRE
Bucknell
Bratoubrya
Lyngam
Presttayne
Litton
Discoyde
Nashe
Pembridg
Lenister
Kyneton
Webley
Glastre
Michaelchurch
Brilley
Clyford cast
Hay
RADNOR
Occidens
BRECNOK
Scala Miliarium
5
10
Burrinton
Orleton
Wigmore c.
Eye
Kinsham
Here: ford
Burford
Midleton
Overhanle
Rochefort
Shelley welshe
Clyston
Whitborne
Wulfer law
Laystas
Kimbalton
Stoke
Hadfeld
Gredon
Edwinloch
Bramyeard
Brodden ham
Bysh fromc
Stokelacye
Rosemaund
Preston
Ingleton
Stretton
Sue Kley
Cowley
Cradley
Easbach
Bosbury
VIGORNIÆ
Calwall
Lidbury
PARS
Oriens
Aylton
Marde. m.
Doriming ton
Wol hope
Bransborugh
Dimmok
Fame hope
Howcaple
Kempley
Newent
Aston
Pars
Rosse
Penyeard
Walford
Glocestriae
Monmouth
Huntisham
Langarran
Hentland
Arcop
Dewchurche mag.
Deuchurche par.
Capul regis
Calow
Kuiston
Eaton
Preston
Wormebridg
Herefo rd
Shelwic
Arcsland
Warton
Wynsley
Hope
Willinton
Cannonpco
Burfeld
Sarnesfeld
Kinersley
Norton
Uinforton
Yasor
Weston
Bredwerdyn
Blakemer
Arcop
Turnaston
Monnynto
Bacton
Llanyhanglees kle
Laveno chap
Clodok
Llantony
The Eothok
Cuntyoye
Langua
Skenfrith cast

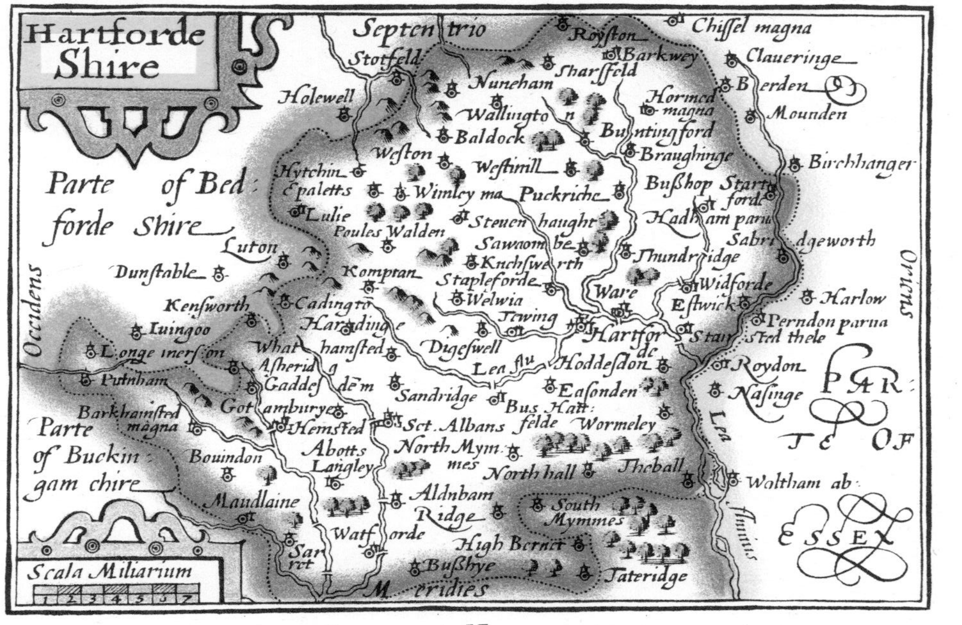
Hartforde Shire
Septentrio
Occidens
Oriens
Meridies
Parte of Bedforde Shire
Parte of Buckingam chire
PARTE OF ESSEX
Scala Miliarium
1 2 3 4 5 6 7
Stotfeld
Holewell
Royston
Barkwey
Chissel magna
Claueringe
Berden
Mounden
Birchhanger
Sharsfeld
Nuneham
Wallington
Baldock
Hormed magna
Buntingford
Braughinge
Weston
Westmill
Hytchin
Epaletts
Wimley ma
Puckriche
Busshop Startforde
Lulie
Steuenhaught
Hadham parua
Sabridgeworth
Poules Walden
Sawoombe
Thundridge
Luton
Knebsworth
Dunstable
Kompton
Stapleforde
Widforde
Welwia
Ware
Estwick
Harlow
Kensworth
Cadington
Tewing
Perndon parua
Iuingoo
Hardinge
Hartforde
Stanstead
Longe merston
Whathamsted
Digeswell
Roydon
Asherige
Lea flu
Hoddesdon
Putnham
Gaddesden
Sandridge
Easonden
Nasinge
Barkhamsted magna
Gotamburye
Bus Hatt
Hemsted
Sct. Albans
Wormeley
Bouindon
Abotts Langley
North Mymmes
North hall
Theball
Lea
Woltham ab
Maudlaine
Aldnbam
Ridge
South Mymmes
Watforde
High Bernet
flumius
Sarret
Busshye
Tateridge

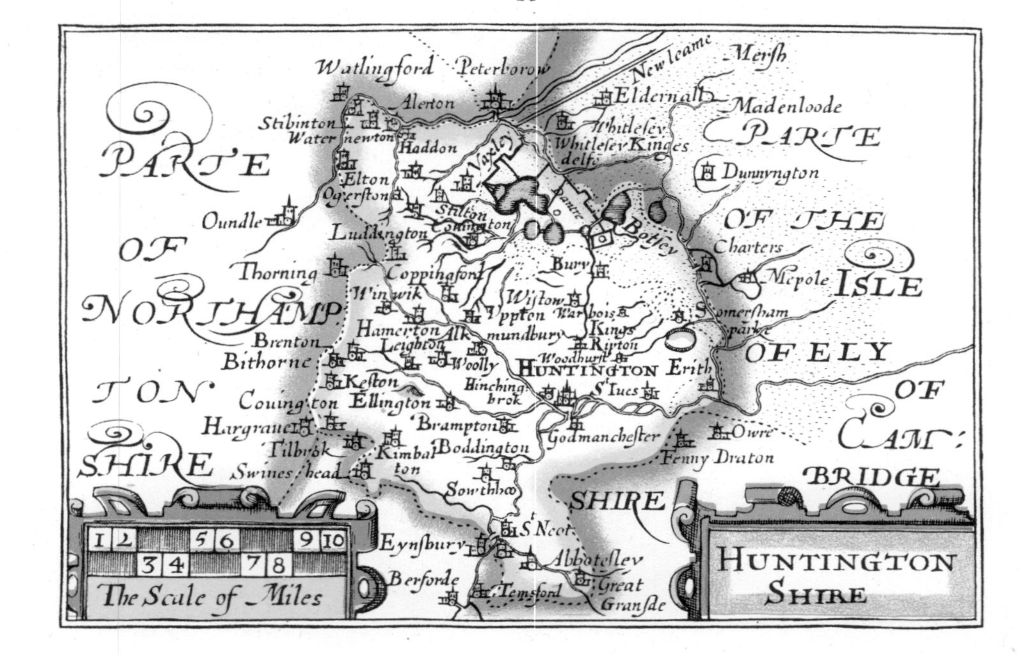
HUNTINGTON SHIRE
The Scale of Miles
1 2 3 4 5 6 7 8 9 10
PARTE OF NORTHAMPTON SHIRE
PARTE OF THE ISLE OF ELY
OF CAMBRIDGE SHIRE
Watlingford
Peterborow
Newleame
Mersh
Eldernall
Madenloode
Alerton
Stibinton
Water newton
Haddon
Whitlesey
Whitlesey Kinges delfe
Dunnyngton
Vaxley
Elton
Ogerston
Oundle
Stilton
Connington
Luddington
Botsey
Charters
Mepole
Thorning
Coppingford
Bury
Winwik
Wistow
Warbois
Vppton
Somersham parke
Hamerton
Alkmundbury
Kings Ripton
Brenton
Leighton
Woodhurst
Bithorne
Woolly
HUNTINGTON
Erith
Keston
Hinching brok
St Iues
Couington
Ellington
Hargraue
Brampton
Godmanchester
Owre
Tilbrok
Kimbalton
Boddington
Fenny Draton
Swineshead
Sowthhoo
St Neot
Eynsbury
Abbotesley
Berforde
Temsford
Great Gransde

KENT
PARTE OF SUSSEX
The Scale of Miles
1 2 3 4 5 6 7 8
LONDON
The Ile of Greane
The Ile of Shepey
ILE OF THANET
Maidston
Rochester
Canterbury
Sandwich
Douer
Folkston
Tunbridge
Grauesend
Dartforde
Feuersham
Ashford
Rumney
Stone end
Dym church
Globesden gut
Whitstable
Winchelsey
Westram

Lancaster
Scala Miliar.
5
10
15
EBORA
OCEANUS
CENSIS PARS
PARS DARBIÆ
Ravsenglas
Eskedale
Arneside
Wenander: mere
Kendale
Blakhall
Seaton
Whitbeck
Grath: wate
Brou ghton
Bouthe
Mylathorp
Kirkbyluncsdale
Millum cas
Vlu erston
Flokesbar: ore
Thur: land
Ingleboro hill
Carn: forth
Hornby cast
Daulton
Barrohead
Tateham chap.
Walney Insula
Ramside
Mydleton
Lancastre
Glason
Barrbye
Gisborn
Garstang
Esington
Mitton
Colne
Hacknsal hall
Roßohall
Longridge cha.
Read
Holme
Byspham m
Plunton
Finstleton
Kirkham
Laton
Marton mere
Preston
Lango
Roßendale
Letum
Blackborn
Walton hall
New hall
Rochodale
Hesket
Laland
Bolton
Meules
Bury
Wigan
Blakerode
Barton
Henton
Watley
Ormiskirk
Bootes hall
Formbye
Max chester
Kilcheth
Mellen
Hughall
Cresby pa
Meller chap
S. Ylyus chap
Ashton
Partinton
Leverpole
Penketh
Stopford
Hale
Warrington

LEICESTER SHIRE
PARTE OF DAR: BIE SHIRE
PARTE OF NOT: TINGHA SHIRE
PARTE OF RUT LAND SHIRE
PARTE OF WARWICK SHIRE
PARTE OF NORTHAMPT
Swalston
Bredon on the hill
Stanton Harald
Blangerby
Ashby de la Zouch
Newton
Tam worth
Hogges norton
Grindon
Poole
Willingcot
Ratcliffe Culey
Ketworth
Hathern
Langley
Dishley grang
Gare
Luton
Longh: borow
Pakinton
Normanton
Heather
Dradgate
Thornton
Orton
Oddston
Cunsto
Newton
Temple
Bosworth
Glensield
Shenton
Gadeby
Braunston
Stapleton
Narborow
Hinckley
Sapcote
Wigs ton litle
Clabrocke
Lulterworth
Radcliff
Kinston
Stanfort
Cotes
Prestwood
Barow
Cussinton
Holwell
Welby
Mountsorell
Leicester
Elston
Emingto
Filton
Launde
Litle Glin
Norto
Tugby
Wiston
Blaby
Sutto
Burto
ouery
W. Lagton
Armesby
Knaptost
Kimcot
Harburgh
Shauell
Newton
Lilborne
Rugby
Stanfor
Litle Boude
Reasby
Pickwel
Crawsto
Tuiford
Somerby
Sutton
Barsto
Rodmel
Langer
Stathern
Melton mowbray
Eton
Waltham on the would
Normanton
Muston
Beuer Cast
Braunston
Croxton
Buckminster
Saxby
Tighe
Lagham
Braunston
Broke
Alexton
Wanlton
Caucott
Hall erton
Holt
Welha
Weston
Rokingham Cast
1 2 3 4 5 6 7 8 9 10
A Scale of Miles

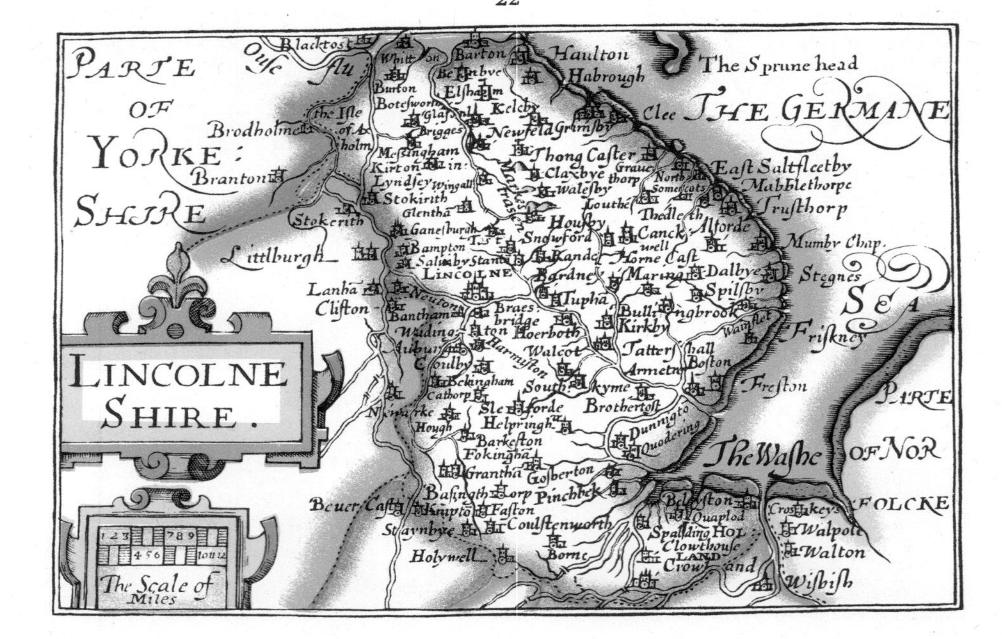
LINCOLNE SHIRE.
PARTE OF YORKE: SHIRE
THE GERMANE SEA
PARTE OF NORFOLCKE
The Washe
The Sprune head
The Scale of Miles
1 2 3 4 5 6 7 8 9 10 11 12
Ouse
Blacktost
Brodholme
Branton
Stokerith
Littlburgh
Lanha
Clifton
Beuer Castle
Staynbye
Holywell
Barton
Haulton
Habrough
Clee
Kelby
Newfeld
Grimsby
Thong Caster
Claxbye
Walesby
Messingham
Kirton in Lyndsey
Stokirith
Glentha
Ganesburgh
Bampton
Houlby
Snowford
LINCOLNE
Bardney
Tupha
Horne Cast
East Saltfleetby
Mabblethorpe
Trusthorp
Alforde
Mumby Chap.
Dalbye
Stegnes
Spilsby
Frisknеy
Kirkby
Tattershall
Boston
Freston
Walcot
Harmiston
Brothertoft
Sleeforde
Helpringham
Barkeston
Fokingha
Grantha
Gosberton
Pinchbek
Dunnigto
Quodering
Coulstenworth
Borne
Spalding
Walpole
Walton
Wisbish

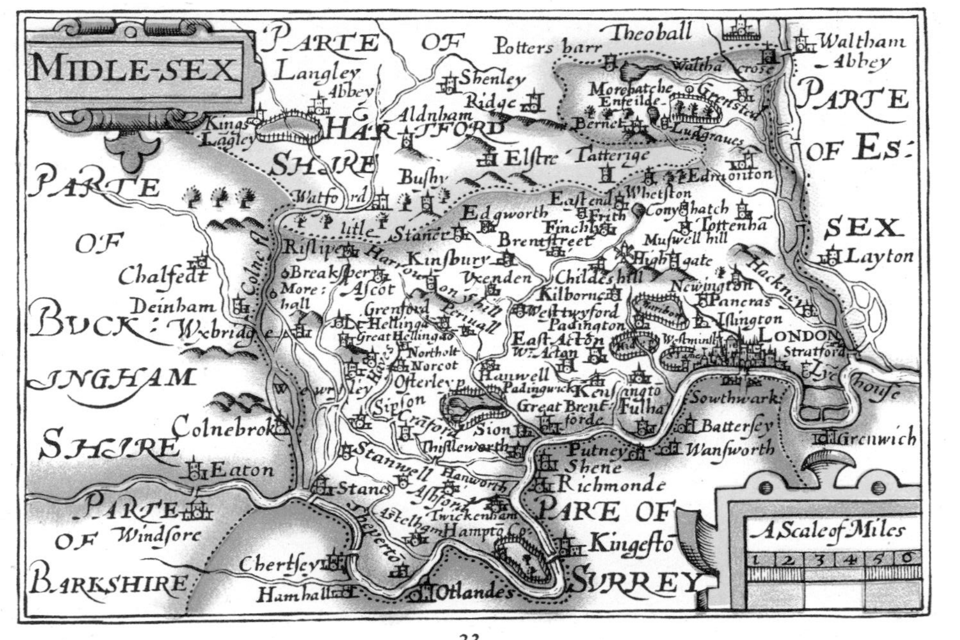
MIDLE-SEX
PARTE OF HARTFORD SHIRE
Langley Abbey
Kings Lagley
Potters barr
Theoball
Waltham Abbey
Waltha crose
Shenley
Ridge
Aldnham
Morehatche
Enfeilde
Grensted
Bernet
Ludgraues
Elstre
Tatterige
Edmonton
Bushy
Watford
PARTE OF ES: SEX
Layton
PARTE OF BUCK: INGHAM SHIRE
Chalfedt
Deinham
Wxbridge
Colne fl
Colnebrok
Eaton
PARTE OF Windsore
BARKSHIRE
East end
Whetston
Frith
Cony hatch
Tottenha
Edgworth
Finchly
Muswell hill
litle Stanee
Brentstreet
High gate
Hackney
Rislipe
Harrow on hill
Kinsbury
Vxenden
Childes hill
Newington
Breakspere
More: hall
Ascot
Kilborne
Paneras
Islington
Grenford
Perivall
West twyford
Padington
LONDON
Stratford
Helling
Great Hellingdō
East Acton
Westminster
Northolt
Norcot
W. Acton
Hanwell
Otterley p.
Padingwick
Kensingto
Southwark
Sipson
Great Brentforde
Fulha
Crafford
Sion
Battersey
Grenwich
Thistleworth
Wansworth
Putney
Shene
Richmonde
Stanwell
Hanworth
Stanes
Ashford
Twickenham
PARE OF SURREY
Kingesto
Astelham
Hampto Co.
Sheperto
Chertsey
Hamhall
Otlandes
A Scale of Miles
1 2 3 4 5 6

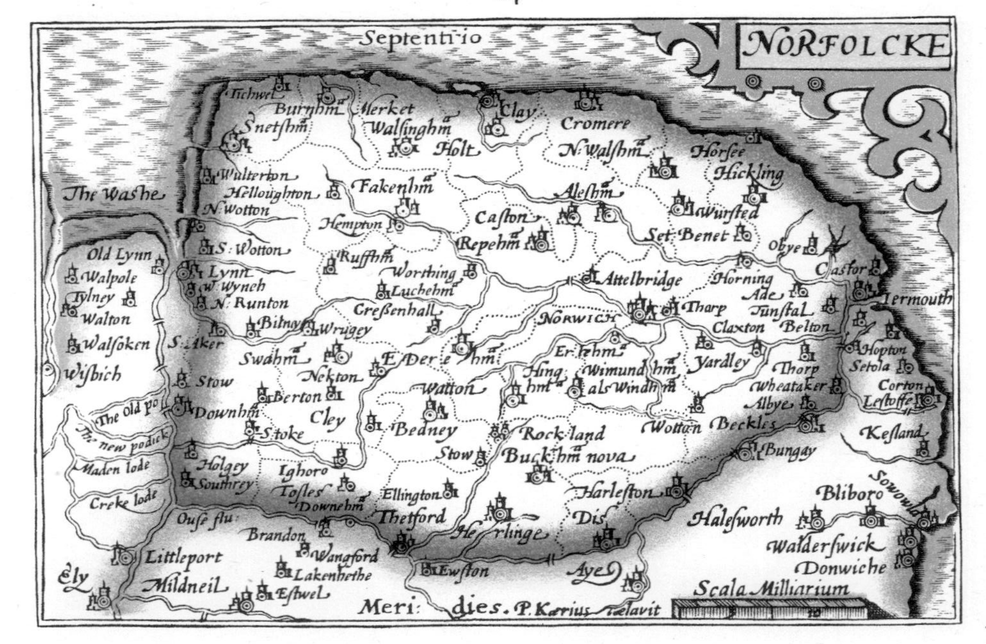
NORFOLCKE
Septentrio
The Washe
Old Lynn
Walpole
Tylney
Walton
Walsoken
Wisbich
The old po
The new podick
Maden lode
Creke lode
Ouse flu:
Ely
Littleport
Mildneil
Brandon
Wangford
Lakenhethe
Estwel
Tichwel
Burnhm
Snetshm
Merket
Walsinghm
Clay
Holt
Cromere
N: Walshm
Horsee
Hickling
Wulterton
Helloughton
N: Wotton
Fakenhm
Hempton
Aleshm
Caston
Repehm
Wursted
Set: Benet
Obye
Castor
S: Wotton
Lynn
W: Wyneh
N: Runton
Bilney
Russhm
Worthing
Luchehm
Gressenhall
Wrugey
Attelbridge
Horning
Ade
Tunstal
Belton
Tharp
Claxton
Iermouth
NORWICH
Swahm
Nekton
E: Der e hm
Er: lehm
Hing: hm
Wimund hm als Windh m
Yardley
Thorp
Wheataker
Albye
Hopton
Setola
Corton
Lestoffe
Stow
Downhm
Berton
Cley
Stoke
Watton
Bedney
Rock land
Buck hm nova
Wotton
Beckles
Kesland
Bungay
Stow
Holgey
Southrey
Ighoro
Tosles
Downehm
Ellington
Thetford
Herlinge
Harleston
Dis
Halesworth
Bliboro
Sowowld
Walderswick
Donwiche
Ewston
Aye
Scala Milliarium
Meri: dies. P. Kærius cælavit

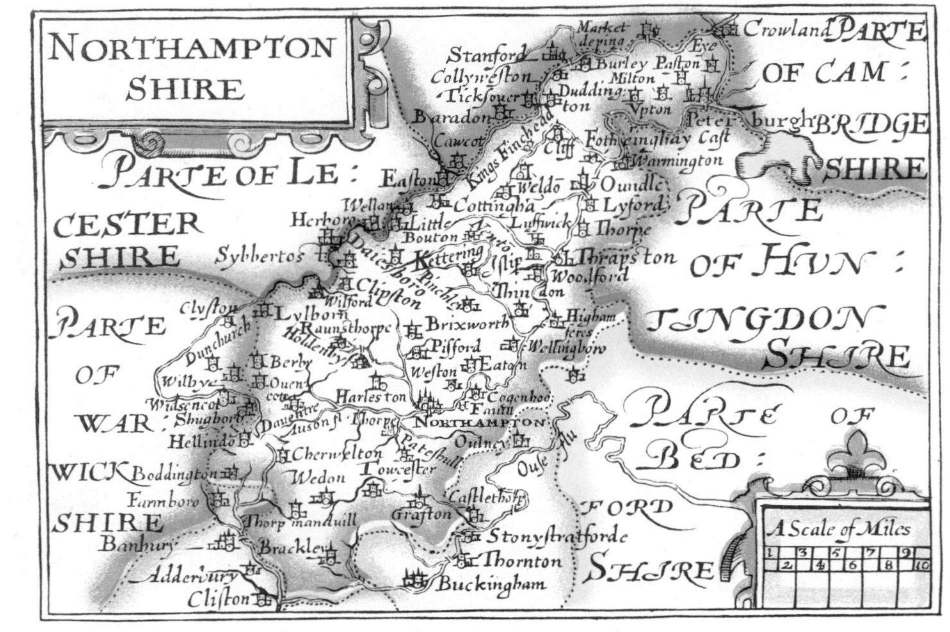
NORTHAMPTON SHIRE
PARTE OF LE:
CESTER
SHIRE
PARTE
OF
WAR:
WICK
SHIRE
Crowland
PARTE
OF CAM:
BRIDGE
SHIRE
PARTE
OF HUN:
TINGDON
SHIRE
PARTE OF
BED:
FORD
SHIRE
Market deping
Stanford
Collyweston
Ticksouer
Dudding ton
Burley
Paston
Eye
Milton
Vpton
Peter burgh
Baradon
Cawcot
Kings Finchead
Cliff
Fotheringhay Cast
Warmington
Easton
Weldo
Oundle
Wellan
Cottingha
Lyford
Herboro
Little Bouton
Luffwick
Thorpe
Sybbertos
Daiesboro
Kettering
Islip
Thrapston
Woodford
Clipston
Pinchley
Thrindon
Wilsford
Clyston
Lylborn
Higham feres
Raunsthorpe
Brixworth
Holdenby
Dunchurch
Pisford
Wellingbow
Berby
Weston
Eaton
Willbye
Ouencote
Harleston
Cogenhoo
Faxton
Widsencot
Daventre
Shugboro
Auson
Thorpe
NORTHAMPTON
Hellindo
Cherwelton
Pateshull
Oulney
Ouse flu
Boddington
Wedon
Toucester
Farnboro
Castlethorpe
Thorp manduill
Grafton
Banbury
Brackley
Stonystratforde
Thornton
Adderbury
Buckingham
Cliston
A Scale of Miles
1 2 3 4 5 6 7 8 9 10

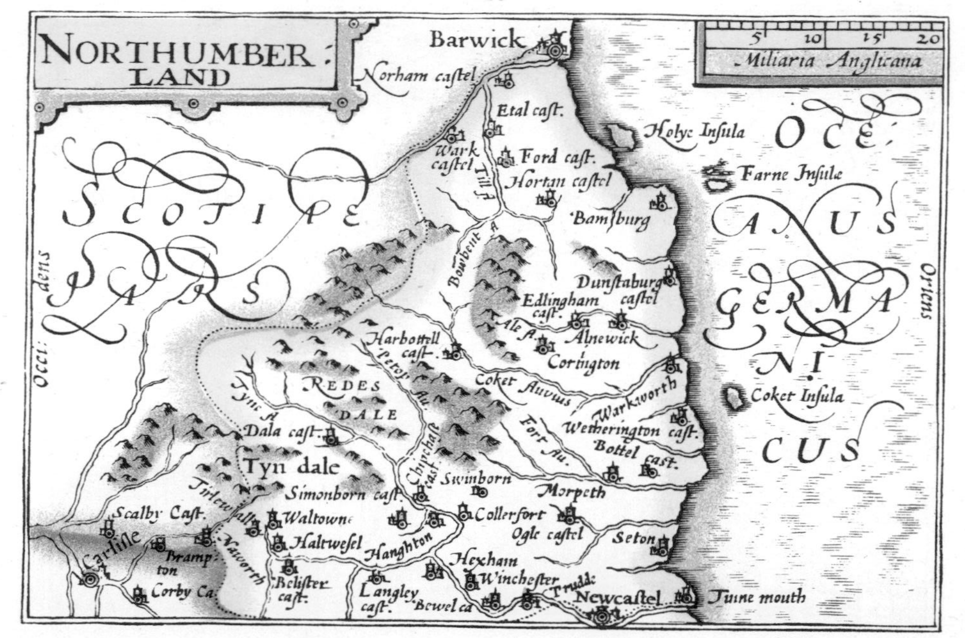
NORTHUMBER: LAND
Barwick
Norham castel
Etal cast.
Wark castel
Ford cast.
Till A
Hortan castel
Bamsburg
Holye Insula
Farne Insule
OCEANUS GERMANICUS
SCOTIAE PARS
Occi: dens
Oriens
5 10 15 20
Miliaria Anglicana
Bowbent A
Dunstaburg castel
Edlingham cast.
Ale A.
Alnewick
Cortington
Harbottell cast.
Petos Au.
Coker Auvius
Warkworth
Coket Insula
Wetherington cast.
Bottel cast.
Fort Au.
REDES DALE
Tyne A
Dala cast.
Tyn dale
Chipchase cast.
Swinborn
Morpeth
Simonborn cast.
Collerfort
Ogle castel
Seton
Tirlewall
Waltowne
Haltwesel
Hanghton
Hexham
Winchester
Trudd:
Newcastel
Tine mouth
Scalby Cast.
Carlisle
Brampton
Naworth
Corby Ca
Belister cast.
Langley cast.
Bewel ca

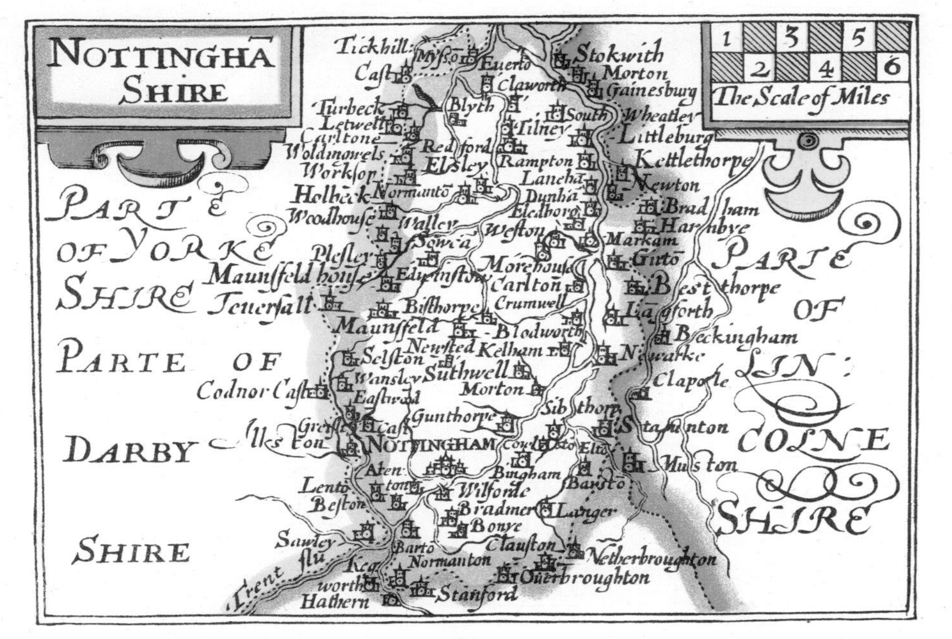

NOTTINGHA SHIRE
1 2 3 4 5 6
The Scale of Miles
PARTE OF YORKE SHIRE
PARTE OF DARBY SHIRE
PARTE OF LIN: COLNE SHIRE
Tickhill
Cast
Mysso
Euerto
Stokwith
Morton
Gainesburg
Claworth
Turbeck
Letwell
Carltone
Woldinowels
Worksop
Blyth
South
Wheatley
Tilney
Littleburg
Redford
Elsley
Rampton
Kettlethorpe
Laneha
Newton
Holbeck
Normanto
Dunha
Woodhouse
Walley
Eledborg
Bradham
Weston
Harnbye
Sowca
Markam
Plesley
Morehouse
Maunsfeld house
Edwinstow
Carlton
Teuersall
Bisthorpe
Crumwell
Maunsfeld
Blodworth
Beckingham
Newsted
Selston
Kelham
Suthwell
Wansley
Clapole
Codnor Cast
Eastwad
Morton
Gunthorpe
Sibthorp
Greisly
Cast
Ilkston
NOTTINGHAM
Bingham
Muston
Aten
ton
Lento
Beston
Wilforde
Bradmer
Langer
Bonye
Sawley
Trent flu
Barto
Normanton
Clauston
Netherbroughton
Keg
worth
Hathern
Stanford
Ouerbroughton

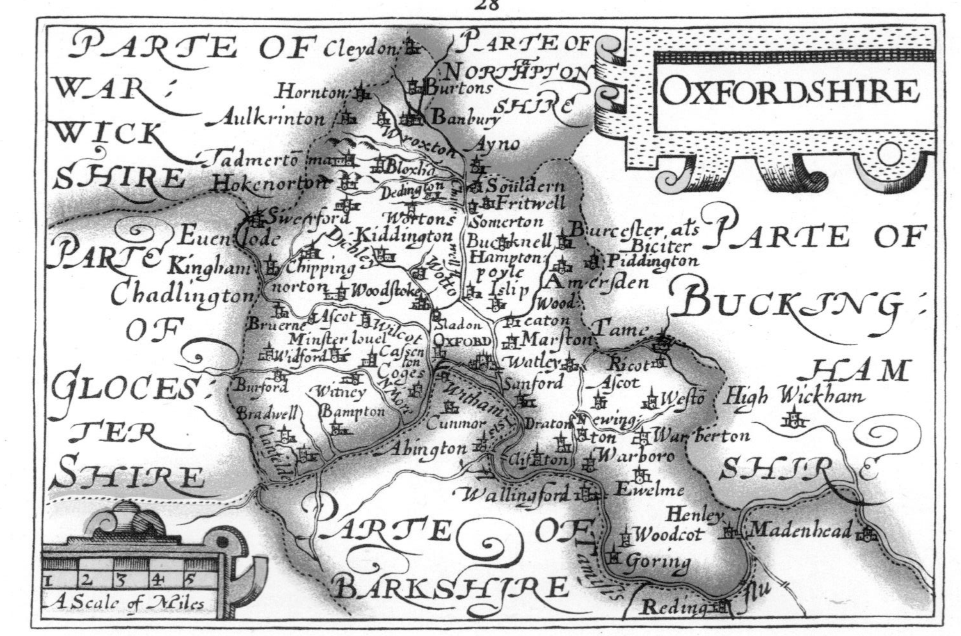
OXFORDSHIRE
PARTE OF WAR: WICK SHIRE
PARTE OF NORTHAPTON SHIRE
PARTE OF BUCKING: HAM SHIRE
PARTE OF GLOCES: TER SHIRE
PARTE OF BARKSHIRE
Cleydon
Hornton
Burtons
Aulkrinton
Banbury
Wroxton
Ayno
Tadmerto
Hokenorton
Bloxha
Dedington
Souldern
Fritwell
Swerford
Wortons
Somerton
Euenlode
Kiddington
Bucknell
Burcester, als Biciter
Kingham
Chipping norton
Dichley
Hampton poyle
Piddington
Amersden
Chadlington
Woodstoke
Wotto
Islip
Wood
Ascot
Wilcot
Sladon
Bruerne
Minster louel
OXFORD
Marston
Tame
Widford
Cassenton
Watley
Ricot
Burford
Witney
Coges
Sanford
Ascot
Westo
High Wickham
Bradwell
Bampton
Witham
Cunmor
Draton
Newington
Warberton
Clanfelde
Abington
Clifton
Warboro
Wallingford
Ewelme
Henley
Woodcot
Madenhead
Goring
Reding
Tamisis flu
1 2 3 4 5
A Scale of Miles

RVTLANDE SHIRE
PARTE OF LINCOLNE SHIRE
PARTE OF LECES: TER SHIRE
PARTE OF NORTHAMPTON SHIRE
Edmundthorp
Market Ouerton
Clipsham
Pickworth
Stretton
Hardwick
Ezenden
Ryall
Belmisthorpe
Rollors stone
Tholthorp
Horne
Cotsmore
Wenton
Ashwell
Langh
Burley
Whitwel
Catmouse mill
Colld ouerton
Knaston
OVKHAM
Braunston
Edgton
Gunthorp
Epingham
STANFORD
Little Casterton
Normanton
Timwell
Newbottle
Burghley
Edyweston
Lindo
North Luffeham
Ketton
Manton
Martinsthorp
Leelodge
The Kings lodge
Brook
Withcock
Laund
Fregthorp
Geeston
Kelthorpe
Coliweston
Didington
Tixouer
Ridlington
Wing
Preston
Pilton
Tosters bridge
South Luffingham
Moorecot
Lumley lodge
Aiston
Glaiston
Becon hill
Barough don
Waggerley
Ashegate
Belton
Hermitage
Bisbrook
Wardley
Uppingham
Redgate
Seyton
Stokerston
Liddington
Bradgatt
Thorp
Stoke
Snewton
Beehill
Caldecot
The Scale of Miles
1 2 3 4 5 6

Shropshire
The Scale of English Miles
5 10
Petrus Kærius cælavit
Septentrio.
Oriens
Occidens
DENBIGH PARS.
STAFFOR: DIAE PARS
WOR CES: TRIAE PARS
MONTGO: MERYE PARS
SHROWES BURYE
Whitchurche
Oswestr
Wellynton
Newport
Bridgenorthe
Ludlow
Bewdeley
Montgomerye
Bisshops castle
Knighton
Tenburye
Sabrina fluvius

SOMERSET SHIRE
Miliaria Anglicana
5
10
Petrus Kærius cælavit
Septentrio
Occidens
Oriens
Meridies
Bri stoll
Gloc es triæ pars.
WILTONIÆ PARS
PARS DORCESTRIÆ
PARS DEVONIAE.
Flatholms Insula
Stepeholms Insula
Barrowe
Porshut point
Porshut
Walton
Clevedon
Clopton
Wike
N Stoke
Box
Bradford
Canesham
Pensford
Wrinton
Axbridge
Berrinton
Uphill
Hutton
Weston super mare
Worle
Benager
Wells
Wike
Melles
Fronme Selwood
Sheptonmallet
Mylton
Bruton
Gedney
Glassenbury
Meare
Walton
Bridgewater
Huntspill
Mark
Wokey
Gedney more
Chelton
Somerton
Langport
Milton
Muchenay
Taunton
Alford
Pitcomb
Blakford
Quene Camel
Sherborne
Evill
Martok
Ilmister
Charol
Danny
Ilton
Wellington
Runton
Baunton
Tollande
Combe
Spaxton
Enmore
Durlay
Cannington
Comadge
Lystoke
Kulac
Watchet
Duneter
Wyllyton
Luxboro
Exton
Winesford
Mynhead
Por lok
Cure
Dulverton
Upton
Wyveles comb
Crokehornie
West Chenock
Wes t
Caucor

Staffordshhir

Scala Milliarium

5 10 15

Septentrio.

Meridies.

CESTRIÆ PARS.

DARBIÆ PARS

SALOPIAE PARS.

LECESTRIAE. PARS.

WARW PARS

P. Kærius cælavit

Erles bothe
Starndale
Hartington
Wulscot
Tissinton
Ashborne
Bolsley
Congleton
Swithamley
Biddle
Leike
Gryn
New chap
Schedleton
Cawton
Church Lauton
Audley
Norton
Hilton
Barthumlegh
New castel
Betley
Cliton
Calwich
Roncester
Doveridge
Sidbury
Eggington
Bradley
Hanford
Knyghton
Walton
Stone
Uttoxiter
Faulde
Trent flu.
Mukleston
Mar
Eklesha
Sandon mag
Weston
Pagetz bramlay
Burton
Draton
Adbaston
Stafford
Hawood mag
Wichnor
Gnaphal
Raynton
S. Rubboro
Aderswaies
Catton
Pilston
Gnasha
Drayton
Chestall
Newport
Lychfelde
Hamerwicke chap
Tamworth
Worley mag
Sheryshales
Brewood
Walsalt
Dratonbasset
Tetnal
Boyngale
Sutton cosfeld
Shypley
Wulverhampton
Peryhal
Harborn
Gattaker
Amberote
Bromicham
Bublinton
Sturbridge
Starton cast
Raiesley
Hagley
Church hyll
Baryate
Kedermyster

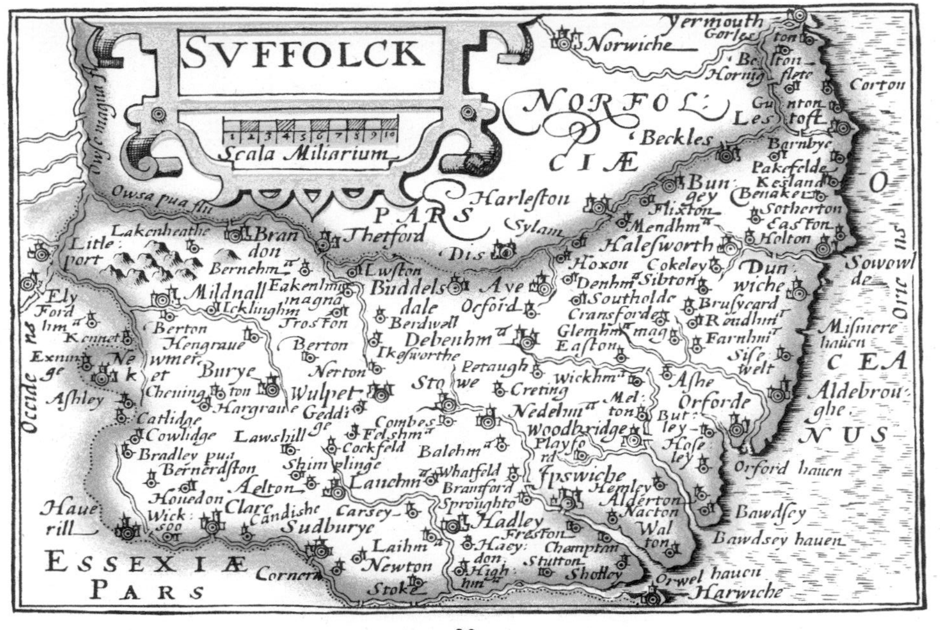
SVFFOLCK
Scala Miliarium
1 2 3 4 5 6 7 8 9 10
NORFOLCIÆ PARS
ESSEXIÆ PARS
OCEANUS
Occidens
Orient
Norwiche
Yermouth
Beckles
Harleston
Thetford
Bungey
Halesworth
Dunwiche
Aldebroughe
Orforde
Woodbridge
Ipswiche
Hadley
Sudburye
Clare
Burye
Wulpet
Debenhm
Buddelsdale
Mildnall
Brandon
Lakenheathe
Newmerket
Hauerill
Harwiche
Orwel hauen
Bawdsey hauen
Orford hauen
Corton
Lestoft
Stowe
Lauenhm
Newton
Stoke

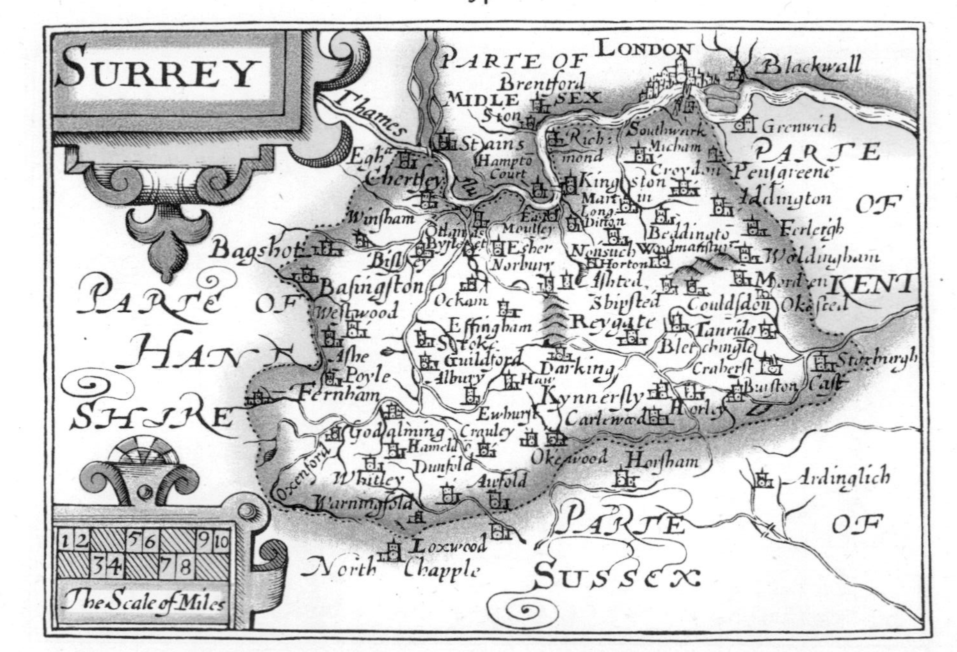
SURREY
PARTE OF MIDLE SEX
LONDON
Blackwall
Brentford
Ston
Thames
Stains
Hampto Court
Rich: mond
Southwark
Micham
Grenwich
PARTE OF KENT
Pensgreene
Addington
Croydon
Kingston
Egham
Chertsey
Winsham
Bagshot
Bisley
Basingston
Westwood
Ashe
Poyle
Fernham
PARTE OF HAN SHIRE
Esher
Norbury
Nonsuch
Horton
Ashted
Shipsted
Reygate
Ockam
Effingham
Stoke
Guildford
Albury
Darking
Beddingto
Woldingham
Ferleigh
Couldsdon
Tanrida
Bletchingle
Craberst
Starburgh Cast
Okested
Kynnersly
Carlewood
Horley
Ewhurst
Crauley
Godalming
Dunfold
Awfold
Okewood
Horsham
Whitley
Warningfold
Oxenford
Loxwood
North Chapple
Ardinglich
PARTE OF SUSSEX
1 2 3 4 5 6 7 8 9 10
The Scale of Miles

SUSSEX
PART OF SURREY
PART OF KENT
The Scale of Miles
THE BRITTISH SEA
Asburst
East Grinsted
Fawhurst
Worth
Hartfeld
Rudgwick
Horsha
Ardingleigh
Mayfeild
Buckhurst
Itchingham
Newnden
Slincha
Sidney
Nelland
Fleteling
Bucksted
Burwash
Warbleton
Beckley
Munfeild
Vdmore
Rye
Oxney Iland
Petworth
Fernhurst
Cowdray
Shipley
Billinshurst
Bulbsoro
Dichling
Hethfeld
Eatwood
Battle
Winchelsey
Crawhurst
Catsfeild
Ore
Old Winchelsey drowned
Hastings
Bevill
Hoo
Havlsham
Hellingle
Crawle
Chaunto
Barcombe
Lewis
Furle
Foynton
Pemsey
Willington
East Dean
Seaforde
Mychling
Brighthelmeston
New Shorham
Poynings
Stening
Kymer
Parham
Coates
Bury
Haughton
Arundel Cast
Torrington
Terring
Limister
Hampton
Midleton
Trefford
Midhurst
Compton
Bepton
Binderton
Stetington
Bockton
CHICHESTER
Dunnington
Pagham
Selsey

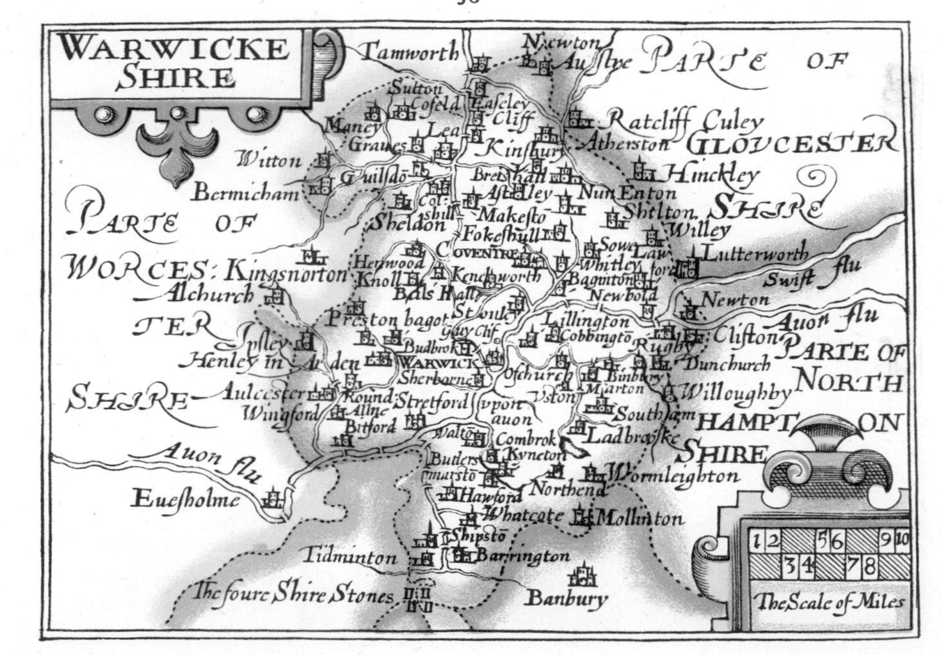
WARWICKE SHIRE
Tamworth
Newton
Austye
PARTE OF GLOUCESTER SHIRE
Sutton Cofeld
Easeley
Cliff
Maney
Graues
Lea
Kinsbury
Ratcliff
Culey
Atherston
Witton
Guilsdō
Bretshall
Astley
Nun Eaton
Hinckley
Bermicham
Col: shill
Makesto
Shelton
Sheldon
Fokeshull
Willey
PARTE OF WORCES: TER SHIRE
Kingsnorton
Coventre
Sowe
Law ford
Lutterworth
Herwood
Knoll
Kenelworth
Whitley
Baginton
Newbold
Swift flu
Alchurch
Bals Hall
Stonley
Newton
Preston bagot
Lillington
Cobbingtō
Auon flu
Guy Clif
Rugby
Clifton
Ipsley
Budbrok
Henley in Arden
WARWICK
Dunchurch
PARTE OF NORTH HAMPTON SHIRE
Sherborne
Ofchurch
Binbury
Aulcester
Round: Allne
Stretford vpon auon
Vston
Marton
Willoughby
Wingford
Southam
Bitford
Walton
Combrok
Ladbrooke
Auon flu
Butlers marstō
Kyneton
Wormleighton
Northend
Euesholme
Hawford
Whatcote
Mollinton
Shipstō
Tidminton
Barrington
The foure Shire Stones
Banbury
1 2 3 4 5 6 7 8 9 10
The Scale of Miles

WILT SHIRE
Parte of Glocester Shire
Parte of Somerset Shire
Occidens
Oriens
Parte of Ham
Scala Miliari
5
10
Tetbury
Malmesbury
Bathe
Bradford
Frome
Calne
the Devyses
Salesbury
Farrindon
Lambourne
Hungerforde
Swindon
Shaftesbury

Worcestershir
Staffordiæ Pars
Septentrio
Here for diæ Pars
Warw Pars
Oxon. Pars
Occidens
Meridies
Scala Miliarium
5 10
Worcester
Kedermistr
Stirbridge
Edgebaston
Droitwiche
Bromesgroue
Aulcester
Pershore
Tewresbury
Evesholme
Shipton
Sheldon
Helmedon
Solihull
Loxley
Goldecote pk
Lydburie
Upton
Hallow
Martley
Belbroughton
Kingesnorton
Bewdeley
Bayton
Knyghton
Hereford pua
Nether sapye
Whitborn
Stanford
Byshfrome
Easbache
Lulsey
Powick
Pippleton
Harmington
Longdon
Staunton
Pauntley
Bransboring
Bursley
Hampton
Norton
Aulston
Wallersey
Tiddinton

YORK Shire
DUNELMENSIS EPISCOPATUS PARS
OCEANUS
Lincolniae pars
Milliaria Anglica
5 10 15
The toure
Flamborough head
Abborn chapell
Hornsey beck
Mapleton
The sprun head
Grimsby
Hausegarthe
Newton
YORK
Beverley
Wetherby
Rippon
Darlington
Ledes
Wakefelde
Staley
Glassop
Stopfurth
Settle
Colne

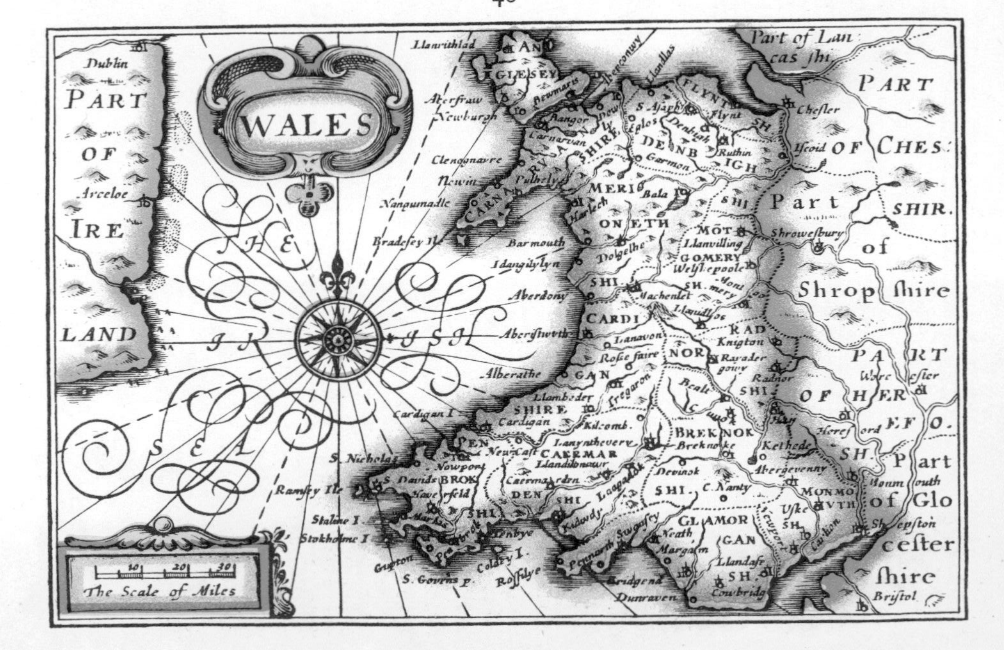
WALES
PART OF IRE LAND
Dublin
Arceloe
THE IRISH SEA
The Scale of Miles
10 20 30
Part of Lancas shi
PART OF CHES:
SHIR.
Part of Shrop shire
PART OF HER EF O.
Part of Glo cester shire
Chester
Shrowesbury
Bristol
ANGLESEY
FLYNT SH
DENBIGH
MERIONETH SHI
MOTGOMERY SH.
CARNARVAN SHIRE
CARDIGAN SHIRE
RADNOR SHI
BREKNOK SHI.
PEN BROK SHI.
CAERMAR DEN SHI
GLAMOR GAN SH.
MONMOVTH SH.
Barmouth
Aberdony
Aberistwith
Alberathe
Cardigan I
S. Nicholas
Ramsey Ile
Stokholme I
S. Govens P.
Dunraven